Being A Wounded Healer

How To Heal Ourselves
While We Are Healing Others

Jessica
Keep caring

Being
A Wounded Healer

How To Heal Ourselves
While We Are Healing Others

Douglas C. Smith

P-S
P

Psycho-Spiritual Publications
Madison, Wisconsin

"When we become aware that we do not have to escape our pains, but that we can mobilize them into a common search for life, those very pains are transformed from expressions of despair into signs of hope." - Henri Nouwen, The Wounded Healer.

"The doctor can put over his authority with fairly good results on people who are easily gulled. But for critical eyes it is apt to look a little too threadbare. . . . It is his own hurt that gives the measure of his power to heal." - Carl Jung, The Practice of Psychotherapy.

"Healing comes not because one is whole, integrated, and all together, but from a consciousness breaking through dismemberment." - James Hillman, "Puer's Wound and Ulysses' Scar."

Douglas C. Smith
Psycho-Spiritual Publications
601 N. Segoe Road, Suite 305
Madison, Wisconsin 53705

Printed in the United States of America

ISBN 0-9672870-0-6

Contents

Woundedness

During the last ten years, my work has allowed me to witness many people going through phenomenal growth. I have observed these people having periods of immense fulfillment. I have seen them experience profound moments of healing. My work has been with the terminally ill.

The terminally ill often see their children coming to them, sharing with them, crying with them, holding them; some healing takes place in those meetings. The terminally ill often see their spouses conveying love in the strongest way they have ever conveyed it; some healing takes place because of that love. The terminally ill often make great discoveries about what is really important in this world; some healing occurs as a result of those discoveries. They often see their faith climbing to new heights never before reached; some healing happens at those heights.

In calling all of the above healing, I am not speaking of a healing that involves erasing problems. I am referring to a healing that has more to do with being open to our problems, facing them, and realizing that much can be gained in the midst of them. I am not referring to a healing that comes through the elimination of woundedness, but a healing that comes while still having woundedness.

This possibility of healing in the midst of woundedness is not confined to the unmistakable pain and suffering of dying; healing can be found in all kinds of pain and suffering. Healing can be found in the midst of the woundedness of job loss. In the midst of the woundedness of divorce. The woundedness of grief. The woundedness of depression. The woundedness of physical handicaps. Without running away from that woundedness, without hiding from that woundedness, without ignoring that woundedness, healing can take place.

This finding of healing in the midst of woundedness has been very important to me, both personally and professionally. Personally, I have had to struggle with the death of one of my daughters, a lengthy stay in a mental hospital, the renunciation of my priesthood, a divorce, and several other serious wounds. Professionally, as a hospice worker, a minister, and a therapist, I have certainly had to assist people facing many forms of pain and suffering. Being able to find healing within woundedness, without having to have woundedness disappear, has been of great benefit to me as well as to those I have tried to serve.

Personally and professionally, I have come to realize that there is much pain and suffering that does not get eliminated, some suffering that cannot ever be eliminated. That being the case, the possibility of finding healing in the midst of that pain and suffering is of great value, very great value.

The finding of healing in the midst of woundedness is talked about throughout the literature of our spiritual traditions. All the major spiritual traditions make clear arguments for finding healing within pain, suffering, and even death.

In Buddhism, it was the Buddha's witnessing of pain, suffering, and death that was the catalyst for him to renounce all that his life had been up until that point (financial wealth, social prestige, and political importance). The witnessing of pain, suffering, and death led him away from his former life to a far more meaningful life, the life of enlightenment. Without the pain, suffering, and death, Buddha would have never found enlightenment.

Within the Jewish tradition, crucial stories of the early development of that faith center around the important fulcrum of pain, suffering, and death: Adam and Eve, Cain and Abel, Noah and the flood, the sacrifice of Isaac, Jacob's wrestling at Peniel, the Egyptian captivity, the exodus across the desert. During those times of pain, suffering, and death, the Jewish people experienced some kind of transforming healing in the midst of their woundedness. The Jewish people found their strength during those times, before the promised land.

In Christianity, Jesus' pain, suffering, and death revealed the whole purpose of his existence: resurrection, eternal life, permanent healing. Without the pain, suffering, and death, there could be no resurrection, no eternal life, no healing.

Ramana Maharshi, the Hindu teacher, spoke very succinctly of finding healing in the midst of woundedness:

"Your glory lies where you cease to exist." [1] In other words, Hindu thought proclaims that only when we have lost everything that we think is meaningful, will we discover what truly is meaningful: gain is to be found in the midst of loss.

With the same succinctness as Ramana Maharshi, the Muslim teacher Pir Vilayat Inayat Khan said, "Die before death and resurrect now." [2] Gain is to be found in the midst of loss; healing is found in the midst of woundedness.

All of these versions of the woundedness-to-healing message are very puzzling and seem to even defy rationality. However, there must be some very important truth in the woundedness-to-healing message if it has found its way into all of these major spiritual traditions. There must be some very important truth in the message that healing somehow comes from and through pain, suffering, and even death.

Healing does not come from running away from pain, suffering, and death. Healing does not come from ignoring pain, suffering, and death. Healing does not even come from eliminating pain, suffering, and death. Healing comes in the very midst of pain, suffering, and death.

This "spiritual model" is very different from the so-called "medical model." The medical model has the primary goal of "curing," the physical (objective) elimination of a problem. The spiritual model focuses on "healing," the psycho-spiritual (subjective) change in a person that improves the person's quality of life. Cures can come with or without healing; healing can come with or without cures. The medical model concentrates on curing. The spiritual model concentrates on healing, a healing that can occur even if no curing can be found.

Whereas the spiritual model acknowledges that value can come to the wounded and value can even come from woundedness, the medical model aims at somehow eliminating wounds, presenting the possibility of a world where wounds do not have to exist. The medical model focuses on curing. The spiritual model focuses on healing.

Buddha said that the first "noble truth," the very first step towards enlightenment, is the acknowledgement that suffering exists. Pain cannot be erased. We can eliminate our being victimized by that pain, but we cannot eliminate the existence of that pain. According to Buddhist thought, we cannot even begin to proceed down the path that the Buddha offers until we first go through the process of fully accepting suffering, being mindful of it, realizing what causes it, and realizing how to use it to become a more complete individual.

Jesus gave the same message. Jesus said that the path that he offers involves taking up our "crosses" and following him. Notice he did not say to take up our smiles and follow him. Not take up our strengths and follow him. Not our knowledge and degrees. Not the power of positive thinking. We need to take up our crosses (our woundedness, our pain and suffering) and follow him, following his model of using wounds to heal.

The relationship between wounds and healing is so strong within our spiritual traditions that the relationship is often portrayed as being an inseparable one. In Jewish scripture, the book of Job is simultaneously a book portraying unimaginable suffering and a book portraying unshakable faith: the unimaginable suffering brings forth the unshakable faith. The Christian story of the end of Jesus' life is simultaneously a story portraying unimaginable suffering and a story portraying unshakable love: the unimaginable suffering brings forth the unshakable love. Muslim scripture, which portrays several of the same stories portrayed in Jewish and Christian scripture, also speaks of the intertwining of suffering, faith, and love. Both the devotees of Hinduism and Buddhism profess that the journey towards spiritual fulfillment is simultaneously a journey of giving up one thing after another as it is a journey of acquiring one thing after another: the giving up brings forth the acquiring. A central tenet of all of these great spiritual traditions seems to be that pain and suffering, loss and sorrow, even dying and death, carry within them keys that unlock the whole healing process, the essence of spiritual advancement, and the secret to a happy life. Healing is found in the midst of woundedness.

The process of achieving much by giving up much (the process of traveling through woundedness to healing, the process of growing from pain and suffering, the process of passing through death into life) is such a prevalent theme in our spiritual traditions that for many of those traditions there is a specific word or phrase to describe the process. The Hindus call it "moksha." The Buddhists call it "nirvana." The Christians call it "being born again." The Muslims call it "fana."

What each religion is saying (what the spiritual model of care is saying) is that the ultimate way of "living" is a kind of "dying," dying to our self-centeredness, acknowledging our vulnerability, admitting our woundedness, facing our pain and suffering, letting go of what we think is our specialness. A Buddhist would say that "self-negation" is "Self-affirmation." A Christian would say that "dying with Christ" is "rising with Christ."

All of these spiritual teachings are certainly not a celebration of woundedness. Divorce, job loss, depression, physical handicaps are no causes for celebration. There is certainly nothing joyous in pain and suffering.

The core teachings of all of these spiritual traditions claim that that which is not pleasureful, that which is not joyous, can somehow be transformed. Wounds can be used to find healing for oneself. Wounds can be used to help facilitate healing in others.

The medical model as seen in much of modern medicine and modern psychology paints a very different picture. It claims that we can and should eliminate problems. It claims that we can and should escape our wounds. It claims that we do not have to be wounded.

The picture painted by this medical model is very incomplete because not all wounds can be eliminated; there are wounds we cannot escape. Not everyone can recover from a divorce. Not everyone who has lost a job can find a new one. Not everyone who has depression can be cured. Physical handicaps are rarely eliminated. No one escapes the process of dying.

So how do I find healing in the midst of wounds? What about my wounds: how can I find healing in the midst of my own wounds? What about the wounds of others: how can I help others to find healing in the midst of their wounds? How can I experience healing? How can I help others experience healing?

The first step in answering these questions is in realizing that true healing comes in acknowledging and accepting the fact of woundedness. In life, all of us are vulnerable, we all experience physical and emotional suffering, we all can become victimized, we all make errors, and we all have periods of fear, depression, and anger: no philosophy, psychology, or medical intervention can change that. In life, we learn, one way or another, that any attempted avoidance of suffering, mistakes, fear, depression, or anger will only result in more suffering, mistakes, fear, depression, and anger.

Yet, throughout our lives, we have been encouraged to believe that it is important, even desirable, to somehow avoid or escape unpleasant feelings and happenings. Rarely do we ever hear a message about possible gains from exploring difficulties. Rarely do we ever hear about the possibility of learning something from our own unpleasant experiences. Rarely do we ever hear of the possibility of using our unpleasant experiences for some benefit to ourselves and others.

We have been repeatedly taught to not only avoid physical pain, but also many other kinds of unpleasant conditions: boredom, loneliness, restlessness, loss. We have been told that our best interest is served through keeping our distance from all unpleasantness: run from it, hide from it, or pretend that it does not exist. All around us, infomercial barkers are excitedly announcing permanent relief for whatever our ills. All around us, professional models are offering deliverance from any problem we might have. All around us, creative advertising executives are presenting miracle cures for all of our pain and suffering.

Because of this continual conditioning whereby we are told that it is possible to avoid woundedness, we have ended up complicating and magnifying our woundedness. Many of us have become depressed that we are depressed. Many of us have become anxious about our anxiety. Many of us have become angry that we are angry. Many of us have become afraid of our fears. We have often ended up having additional suffering because of the false supposition that there somehow should not be any suffering.

However, when we are realistic about all of the pain and suffering involved in living, we can begin to not be victimized by that pain and suffering. We can begin to discover that our greatest moments of growth are often inseparably linked with our moments of greatest pain and suffering. We can begin to discover that wisdom evolves from conflict. We can begin to discover that maturity is born in crisis. We can begin to discover healing is found in the midst of woundedness.

The world is wounded. Every human experiences problems; no human escapes problems. We all have shortcomings; we all have imperfections. We all experience dissatisfaction. We are all confronted with adversity. We all share in the woundedness of the world. Yet, also, we can all experience healing in the midst of that woundedness, a healing that comes from facing the woundedness.

Let me mention some of my share of the world's woundedness. Let me give you a brief review of my own accumulated pain and suffering, a sort of table of contents for my personal woundedness.

In my childhood, I was continually moving from one home to another, having lived in over fifteen places of residence before I was even fifteen years old, never being able to establish any lasting friendships: I know some things about the woundedness of feeling friendless. When I came to my teenage years, I graduated from high school with a 1.5 grade point average, a D+ average: I know some things about the woundedness of feeling mentally inadequate. Before reaching my mid-twenties, I had lost my first child to death, and before reaching my mid-thirties, I had lost my youngest brother to death: I know some things about the woundedness of losing a loved one to death. At age thirty-eight, I was institutionalized in a mental hospital: I know some things about the woundedness of feeling emotionally and psychologically inadequate. While in the mental hospital, I was asked to renounce my priesthood in the Episcopal Church after being ordained for fourteen years: I know some things about the woundedness of losing a sense of purpose and losing a job, losing a vocation. By age forty, I had experienced divorce: I know some things about the woundedness of going through a divorce and the unwanted separation from one's children. Now, as I begin my fifth decade, I have increasing physical problems. One of those problems is my "familial tremor" that causes me to shake uncontrollably: I know some things about the woundedness of social embarrassment.

Upon hearing all of that, the medical model of care

would say that I am an absolute mess, hardly equipped to be a helper for myself, let alone someone else. The spiritual model of care would say that all of that history of woundedness has provided me with unique gifts for healing. The spiritual model would say that my pains can be "transformed from expressions of despair into signs of hope." [3] The spiritual model would say that I can have a "consciousness breaking through dismemberment." [4] The spiritual model would say that healing can come to me in my woundedness. The spiritual model would even say that healing can come from me because of my woundedness. The medical model says I am an absolute mess and I need to be fixed. The spiritual model says I have a lot of potential!

The Chinese character depicting the word "crisis" has two meanings: danger and opportunity. Our woundedness has two meanings: potential for weakness and potential for strength, potential for further loss and potential for gain. Our wounds pose within themselves a question: will we become diminished at the broken place or greater? I believe every wound, every broken place, provides us with at least two opportunities: the opportunity for us to gain something from that wound and the opportunity for others to gain something from that wound.

In postulating that our own wounds have the ability to not only provide us with healing but also provide others with healing, we are implying that we can experience healing through the woundedness of others. In working with the terminally ill, I have experienced some healing, healing coming from them. I have learned, through them, how to have courage as they have been learning how to have courage. I have learned, through them, the value of touching as they have been learning the value of touching. I have learned, through them, the meaning of love as they have been learning the meaning of love. I have discovered, through them, what is really important in life as they have been discovering what is really important in life. As they have been healing in various ways in the midst of their wounds, I have been healing in various ways through their woundedness.

We must acknowledge the fact that the entire world suffers; woundedness exists with every people of every culture; we all experience pain, suffering, and death. There are many people who have had divorces. There are many people who have had job losses. There are many people who have had loved ones die. There are many people with mental and physical handicaps. There are many people who have experienced violence and abuse. We all have problems; we all have wounds.

Besides acknowledging the existence of our shared woundedness, we have to also acknowledge the potential for some gain from that shared woundedness. There are things we can learn from our own woundedness and there are things we can learn from the woundedness of others. We can grow in the midst of the world's woundedness; we can learn from the world's woundedness; we can heal through the world's woundedness.

We often acknowledge the fact that valuable lessons come from woundedness: think about it. Think of the many ways in which we see value in woundedness.

When it comes to seeking life's teachings, we often prefer to learn from someone with "street" knowledge rather than from someone with just "book" knowledge. In choosing that person with "street" knowledge, we are choosing to learn from someone who has been in the "real" world of pain and suffering, the world of woundedness.

When it comes to seeking out associates or friends, we often seek out people with "depth" in their personalities rather than people with "shallow" personalities. In choosing that person with "depth," we are choosing someone who has had a taste of the real world of pain and suffering, someone with woundedness.

When it comes to seeking a therapeutic relationship with a counselor, minister, social worker, psychologist, nurse, or physician, we often seek out someone who has “first hand” knowledge of our pain, suffering, and woundedness. We want someone who can feel what we feel, someone who has hurt where we hurt, someone who can fully understand our problems and our woundedness.

There are valuable lessons in woundedness. And we seek out people who have learned those valuable lessons.

While I was a patient in a mental institution, I could see in the eyes of many of the other patients “street” knowledge, “depth,” a “first hand” awareness of pain and suffering. Yet, I did not see that in much of the staff; in the staff I saw an ignoring of their own unhealthiness, a hiding from their own woundedness. As a consequence, I and many of the other patients there did not seek healing from many people on the staff. If we wanted to learn anything, change, or grow, we usually sought the assistance of our fellow patients: they were the ones who could really help. We only played games with the staff, the games of pretending, pretending to seek help and pretending to be helped. There could be no healing in the midst of pretending; no healing could come from those who were ignoring and hiding from their own woundedness. For real healing, we sought out those we knew would be willing to acknowledge their own woundedness.

Degrees and titles are of little worth to people who are hurting. If we, as potential helpers, think of our potency as coming from our degrees and titles, our potency is of little worth. Our potency needs to be based upon a rich compost of "street" knowledge, "depth," a "first hand" awareness of woundedness.

As Pema Chodron has said, "Our brilliance, our juiciness, our spiciness, is all mixed up with our craziness and our confusion, and therefore it doesn't do any good to try to get rid of our so-called negative aspects, because in that process we also get rid of our basic wonderfulness." [5] Our pain and suffering is part of our wonderfulness; our wounds are part of our wonderfulness. We can probably even say that without our pain and suffering, without our wounds, we would have no wonderfulness.

The spiritual model says that whenever we become victims of pain and suffering, whether by accident, through someone's malicious intent, through our own errors, or just the result of natural phenomena, we come out of that pain and suffering quite hurt, but also always with some kind of positive potential. The spiritual model says that we can discover through that pain and suffering that we have become beneficiaries of something that has positive possibilities. Through all of our accumulated pain and suffering, we have actually, as difficult as it is to understand, been blessed with something that can be very useful.

There is a mystery here. The mystery is that wounds do not just take away from life; they can add to life as well. Wounds do not have to just take away from who we are; they can add to who we are. Wounds do not have to just take away from what we can do for others; they can add to what we can do for others.

Once again (I need to strongly emphasize the point), I do not wish to belittle pain and suffering: quite the contrary. However, in the midst of all woundedness, we need to see something: potential healing for ourselves and others exists at its very core.

I do not believe we can even relate in any way to someone else's suffering until we first acknowledge our own. We cannot assist in the transformation of someone else's suffering until we first transform our own. We cannot heal someone else until we first know how to heal ourselves. The whole process of healing simply begins with recognizing that we all suffer, we are all wounded. Hinduism recognizes it. Buddhism recognizes it. The Jewish faith recognizes it. The Christian faith recognizes it. The Muslim faith recognizes it. Good psychotherapy recognizes it. Good medicine recognizes it. We start by acknowledging our own woundedness. We enter that woundedness and work through it. By entering that woundedness and working through it, we learn how to heal ourselves and we learn how to assist in the healing of others: healing from and through and with our wounds.

REFLECTION

Write down (or verbally share) the wounds, shortcomings, or problems that your patients, clients, customers, friends or family members bring to you.

Write down (or verbally share) how you gain from their woundedness. How do you grow in the midst of their woundedness?

REFLECTION

Write down (or verbally share) a wound (a loss, imperfection, shortcoming, pain, or suffering) that you carry.

Write down (or verbally share) how you have experienced some growth in your personality as a result of that wound.

Write down (or verbally share) how you might better relate to the woundedness of others as a result of your own woundedness.

Write down (or verbally share) how you feel others might be able to grow as a result of your wound.

REFLECTION

Put together a resume based upon your weaknesses rather than your strengths, listing what your weaknesses qualify you to do and how they equip you to be a better person.

Chapter One
References

1. Ramana Maharshi. (1972). The Spiritual Teaching Of Ramana Maharshi. Boulder, CO: Shambhala.

2. Pir Vilayat Inayat Khan. (1977). Samadhi With Open Eyes. New Lebanon, NY: Messenger Press.

3. Nouwen, H. J. M. (1972). The Wounded Healer. New York: Doubleday.

4. Hillman, J. (1979). "Puer's Wound and Ulysses' Scar." In Puer Papers (pp. 100-128). Dallas: Spring Publications.

5. Pema Chodron. (1991). The Wisdom Of No Escape. Boston: Shambhala.

Healing

In doing hospice work, I have found myself in a rather unusual position within the health care industry: my goal is not to provide a cure. I have expected all of my patients to die while in my care. However, because hospice is not in the business of providing cures, that does not mean that hospice is are not in the business of healing.

"Curing," different from "healing," usually means eliminating a problem. Someone has been cured of cancer, for example, if the cancer is treated in such a way that this person lives as long as she would have lived had she never had that cancer. Someone has received a cure for a broken bone if his bone has been mended in such a way that it is as strong as what it was before the break. Someone has found a cure for depression if she, after receiving treatment for that depression, has no more depressing thoughts than the average person. Curing is an objective elimination of a problem. Finding a cure for someone's particular problem (eliminating that problem) is the goal of the vast majority of health care: the goal of the medical model of care.

Healing (in the way that I choose to define it) is a subjective change that occurs in a person to better equip him or her to address problems in the present and the future: the goal of the spiritual model of care. Healing, as this definition asserts, is more of a qualitative change in a person than a quantitative one.

Healing can often take place even though a cure has not been found. If someone does not find a cure for her cancer, she can still experience some healing in a number of ways: the healing of prioritizing one's values, the healing associated with having a family emotionally reunited, the healing involved in being able to cherish every moment of life as a special gift, the healing coming from developing a strong faith. If someone has a depression that will never be eliminated, she can still experience healing: the healing associated with realizing that there can be purposefulness even within moments of darkness and despair.

Curing of a particular wound implies the elimination of that wound, and healing implies enhancing a person's life even if that wound is not eliminated. Receiving a cure, without healing, could only give us a false security that could easily be shattered when future problems (the same problems or different ones) inevitably arise; healing equips us for those inevitable future problems. Providing someone a cure is like giving that person a welcome gift (which is certainly nice); healing someone is like teaching that person how to find gifts wherever they are (which can be wonderful).

When doing healing work with people, we are not

taking away woundedness because much of what is woundedness can never really be taken away. We cannot eliminate all depression, undo a divorce or a job loss, get rid of all feelings of loneliness, erase a history of persecution and oppression, or ignore our mortality. There has been woundedness in our world and there always will be. However, that is hardly the message we hear all around us: there are people in practically every "helping" profession promising immediate relief, easy answers, miracle remedies. Such is the message of so many psycho-spiritual gurus — the offering of cure-alls when there can be no cure-alls. All around us are people offering cures where there can be no cures and failing to offer healing when there can be much.

An important realization about the healing process is it's circular nature: in helping others, I help myself. In providing others with healing, I provide myself with healing.

When I am trying to help the terminally ill, I am receiving help from them. As they are experiencing healing, I am experiencing healing. We can experience healing for our own woundedness when we are facilitating healing for others in the midst of their woundedness. As Ram Dass and Paul Gorman have said, "We work on ourselves . . . in order to help others. And we help others as a vehicle for working on ourselves." [1]

How then do we facilitate healing in others? For the psychotherapist Carl Rogers there are four conditions that a helper must meet for healing to take place within another. These are what Rogers labels "conditions for growth." [2] They could also be labeled "conditions for healing."

The first condition is called "congruence," an authenticity, an honesty, a showing of ourselves without masks, in all our vulnerability (accepting ourselves with all of our woundedness). Having congruence is being truthful about who we really are.

The second condition is called "empathy," experiencing another's life as if it is our own, experiencing another's suffering as if it is our own suffering, experiencing another's shortcomings as if they are our shortcomings. Being empathic is sharing in the other person's woundedness.

The third condition for growth/healing is what Rogers calls "unconditional positive regard," accepting the other person as worthy of love, accepting someone fully and valuing that person just because that person exists: accepting that person as valuable even with all of that person's hurts, scars, and imperfections.

The fourth condition is to *show* the first three conditions, having the other person directly "experience" the helper's "congruence," "empathy," and "unconditional positive regard." A helper must not just have congruence, empathy, and unconditional positive regard, the helper must show congruence, empathy, and unconditional positive regard.

Using a minor and simple wound for the sake of illustrative purposes, I will show how I experienced some healing with the woundedness that I felt from my poor grade-point average in high school. Someone facilitated that healing for me by possessing the four conditions of growth recommended by Carl Rogers.

I did not initially perceive my poor grades as a problem because I thought that my abilities in the athletic arena would more than compensate for my shortcomings in the cognitive arena. At least that was my perception until I severely injured my shoulder during the final football game of my senior year. After that injury, I could no longer ignore my cognitive shortcomings.

The pain connected with my woundedness of mental inadequacy became most obvious to me on a trip that I made with my dad. He was going to take me from our home in Peoria, Illinois, to colleges throughout the state of Illinois and several of the neighboring states. The intent of the trip was to see what colleges would accept me as a student. Over and over again, we repeated the same ritual: we would drive onto a campus, walk from the car to the admissions office, talk to an admissions officer (my dad doing most of the talking), be told that there was no possibility of me ever being a student there, walk back to the car, and then drive a couple more hours to the next campus to repeat the entire ritual over again. The most painful part of all of that was the car ride between colleges, often spent with much silence, that silence often being filled with me contemplating how much I was disappointing my dad, how ashamed I was in front of my dad who I greatly admired, my dad who had accomplished so much with his life.

Healing for that woundedness of feeling mentally inadequate came through a professor from the University of Minnesota named Bob Blanchard, a man who revealed to me congruence, empathy, and unconditional positive regard. Bob Blanchard allowed me to experience those conditions for growth through a special program that was being offered one summer at Luther College, a small college in Iowa. Bob Blanchard had designed an experimental program for underachieving students, a program designed to motivate students who had shown some potential for further education but had never actualized any of that potential within the traditional academic setting. Twenty-six recent male graduates from high school (or some institution like a high school) were chosen from rather diverse backgrounds: some students had been in juvenile detention centers and jails more than in regular schools, some students had come from Indian reservations without our society's traditional educational programs or testing, and some students got in the program because they had done well on the athletic field but poorly in the classroom (my category).

On that first day of that summer program, the twenty-six of us were expecting our teacher to be some egghead with two inch thick glasses who would stumble into the classroom. We were expecting someone who had no experience with the "real" world, someone who would use words we could not understand, someone who would provide us with a very boring summer. These expectations were dramatically assaulted when Mr. Blanchard marched into the room. With the appearance and stride of a gymnast, he, without saying a single word, marched to the front of the room, stood behind the teacher's desk, took both of his arms and swiped all the books and pencils off the desk, jumped on top of the desk, straightened his legs, and went into a handstand without bending his legs, came down from the handstand with legs still straight, hopped off the desk, and then spoke his first words: "By the end of this summer, everyone of you in this class will be able to do that handstand just as I did it and you will also be able to get straight A's in college. You will be able to do both of those things if you want. But if you are unwilling to set your minds and bodies to doing either of those goals, you might as well leave right now."

My mouth was hanging open; all of us had our mouths hanging open. My immediate thought was, "Is this guy for real?" By the end of that first meeting with Bob Blanchard, I was convinced that he was indeed very "real." He was genuinely excited about excelling physically and intellectually. He lived and breathed excellence, and he was determined to make all of us live and breathe that same excellence. There was nothing false about him; what we saw was what he was; he practiced what he preached; he had authenticity; he had "congruence." After just sixty minutes of portraying his genuine enthusiasm, he made several strenuous reading assignments and dismissed the class for the day.

That night, after spending most of the afternoon talking with the other students, I read for three hours: more reading than I had ever done in an entire week previous to that summer. That night I also spent about twenty minutes making some feeble attempts at duplicating that straight-legged handstand.

The first half of the second day, Mr. Blanchard told us more about his background. He told us about how he used to be teased by neighborhood kids, how they called him weak and dumb, how he had shared the same wound that we shared. He told about all the ways people had made him feel that he was dumb. While he was speaking, I had the feeling that he was not just telling us his story; he was telling the story of everyone else in that room as well. He knew about what it was like to be labeled inferior; he knew about what it was like to be labeled mentally inadequate. I felt his understanding and "empathy" for my shortcomings; I felt that he was on my side; I felt that he and I were of the same stuff.

The second half of that second day, Mr. Blanchard went around the room addressing us each by name and saying some things about each of us and our backgrounds. Apparently, while we had been doing our homework on the previous night, he had been doing his homework, studying each of our admission files. As he told about each of our backgrounds, he mentioned why people outside that classroom might think that we could never do well in college. But then, with each one of us, one at a time, Mr. Blanchard explained why he believed that we could in fact get straight A's in college, giving specific references to our individual histories. He believed in us; he had confidence in us; he had "unconditional positive regard" for all of us. He then concluded that day with more reading assignments.

After class that second day, I went straight to my room and started reading. I read for five hours and forgot to go to dinner. (I had never before forgotten to go to dinner.) I also spent about forty minutes trying to do that straight-legged handstand. After those forty minutes, I was not anywhere close to duplicating Mr. Blanchard's gymnastic feat. However, I did a little better at it than the first night.

Throughout that summer, I missed several dinners because of my new appetite for knowledge. Consequently, I went from my normal football weight of two hundred and ten pounds down to one hundred and seventy-five pounds. The losing of that weight also must have helped me in my flexibility, because the more weight I lost, the closer I got to doing that straight-legged handstand. Of course, the thirty to forty minutes of practice that I was doing every night probably helped a little as well.

By the end of that summer, I did that handstand. By the end of my first semester at college, I had made the Dean's list.

Bob Blanchard did not "cure" my mental deficiencies: there could be no erasing of my poor performance in high school, and my IQ has certainly not gone through some miraculous change. However, Bob Blanchard did teach me how to work with my shortcomings; he did help me to grow even with that quantitatively unchanged IQ. Bob Blanchard did help me improve the quality of my life by giving me an appreciation of knowledge and giving me an awareness that even with my shortcomings I could achieve much. So, if someone gives me an intellectual challenge, I will read twice as much as anyone else while reading at half the typical person's speed. Also, with my mental shortcomings, thanks to Bob Blanchard, I have gotten three masters degrees. I am certainly not "cured" of my less than admirable IQ, but I continue to experience "healing" in those areas, and I am having a lot of fun in that healing.

Of course, this personal story does not illustrate a very serious wound, but it does illustrate a model that can work with all kinds of wounds, serious and not-so-serious. This story illustrates the fact that those who have wounds can experience healing through people who possess "congruence," "empathy," and "unconditional positive regard," the conditions for growth, the conditions for healing.

This woundedness-to-healing process involves a depth of interaction that demands a great amount of maturity. The sharing involved in the woundedness-to-healing process certainly does not mean taking on a shallow psychological exhibitionism ("You think you have got it bad? Let me tell you about my troubles." Or the more subtle form: "I can understand where you're coming from because I have been there."). The sharing involved in the woundedness-to-healing process also does not mean completely abdicating the role of the helper and exploiting someone to do our healing work for us (manipulating people into being our helpers). There is need for a real depth that involves a mature "consciousness breaking through dismemberment," [3] a consciousness that does not have some hidden, self-centered agenda. The depth involves sharing from our own woundedness without any ulterior motives, showing congruence in regard to our own pain and suffering, showing empathy for the pain and suffering of others, and showing unconditional positive regard for those others in the midst of their pain and suffering.

The healing facilitator's first mature expression is congruence, i.e. authenticity. Without congruence, our empathy will not be believed and our unconditional positive regard will not even be heard. If I had not been impressed with Bob Blanchard's authenticity, I would have never begun the journey of healing. If I had not been impressed with Bob Blanchard's honesty about who he really was (what he believed in and how he too was wounded), I would have never begun the journey of healing. This congruence, this authenticity, is the first characteristic of a person wishing to facilitate healing.

What gives us congruence? How do we get it? We certainly do not get it by having many degrees. We also do not get it by having knowledge of how others have been helpers. We do not even get it from having personal experience of being helpful. We get congruence through our humble knowledge of, and humble acceptance of, our own woundedness — not pretending to be without wounds. Our congruence comes from outwardly showing what we inwardly are: a person of imperfections, shortcomings, pain, and suffering.

Any good therapist will admit that he or she cannot change a person. People change themselves; people have to make a conscious choice to change themselves. Also, people will not make that conscious choice until they perceive that there is "a way" for them to go, a way that is achievable given their own woundedness, a way that has been traveled by someone who also has woundedness. A good therapist, through congruence, represents that way; a good therapist is an example of finding healing in the midst of woundedness.

For us to follow "the way" of Jesus' healing message, it helps us to know that he was "bone of our bone, and flesh of our flesh." For any of us to accept the invitation extended to us as those who "travail and are heavy laden," we need to know that the person offering that invitation has also travailed and been heavily laden. Jesus represents a way (an example) of finding healing in the midst of woundedness.

For us to follow "the way" of Buddha's healing message, we need to know that he has suffered as we have suffered, that he has been as disillusioned as we have been disillusioned, that he knows woundedness because he has had woundedness. Buddha represents a way (an example) of finding healing in the midst of woundedness.

"The way" of Judaism's healing message comes through people like Sarah, Abraham, Joseph, Moses, Ruth, David, Job, Jeremiah, Hosea, people who humbly knew pain, poverty, betrayal, loss, despair, sacrifice, and death. Sarah, Abraham, Joseph, Moses, Ruth, David, Job, Jeremiah, and Hosea represent a way (examples) of finding healing in the midst of woundedness.

All of these spiritual traditions show that we will follow the way of someone who is congruent, someone who has experienced emptiness and loss, someone who has been wounded — and does not hide it. We will value and learn from people who are vulnerable as we are vulnerable, people who are on the same level with us, not people who try to somehow elevate themselves up or manipulate us down.

If people have wounds, they are potential healers; if we have wounds, we are potential healers. Every person who has grown as a result of coping effectively with life's tragedies — e.g. experiencing divorce, losing a job, mourning a loved one's death, suffering as a result of sexual abuse, recovering from some addiction, raising a disabled child, adjusting to a physical handicap, struggling with mental illness, etc. — is a potential healer, a potential growth-facilitator for others going through crises. All of us who travail and are heavy laden are potential healers. All of us who have experienced disillusionment are potential healers. All of us who have known pain, poverty, betrayal, loss, despair, sacrifice, or death are potential healers.

Once we have accepted our own woundedness without trying to hide it or use it for some self-centered agenda, and we have become congruent by acknowledging that "our brilliance, our juiciness, our spiciness, is all mixed up with our craziness and our confusion" (our healing potential is all mixed up with our woundedness), we are ready for the next step in the healing process: empathy. Whereas congruence is accepting the fact that each of us is wounded and we live in a world of woundedness, empathy demands a further step: the acceptance and acknowledgment of the fact that we share one another's wounds. With empathy, I feel wounded when others are wounded. With empathy, I feel that I have shortcomings when others have shortcomings. With empathy, I feel with and for others because I cannot distance myself from others; we are inseparable.

With empathy, my sense of "I" becomes tied to a "we." With empathy, my sense of "mine" becomes tied to an "ours." With empathy, my sense of independence is replaced with a sense of interdependence. I live in others and others live in me.

Empathy helps us to not rush to easy answers and illusory cures. With empathy I have to not rush to my readily available thoughts and feelings, but rather must wait for, and listen to, the other's thoughts and feelings. With empathy I also realize that every problem has immense complexity. With empathy we pause in our caregiving to feel the intensity of the other's woundedness, and, in feeling that intensity, we realize that there are no easy answers and there are no instant cures. With empathy, we realize that there are no easy answers for anger, fear, abuse, oppression, pain, longing, anxiety, disappointment, depression, or mourning. However, even though there might not be any easy answers or instant cures for those wounds, empathy helps to facilitate healing for all of those wounds.

The next step in facilitating healing in others (after honestly accepting our own woundedness and honestly accepting the fact that we share in one another's woundedness) is unconditional positive regard, the acceptance of the other person with all of the other's wounds. As empathy is feeling united with the wounds of the other person, unconditional positive regard is feeling united with the person who has those wounds. With unconditional positive regard, we accept and value the other person without judging the other person unworthy of love: no matter what the form of that person's imperfections or shortcomings, no matter what the form of that person's woundedness.

With unconditional positive regard, the other person is as valuable as I am valuable. With unconditional positive regard, I realize that the other is someone whose woundedness is just as important as my woundedness and whose potential for healing is just as great as my potential for healing. With unconditional positive regard, the other person has unquestionable, undeniable value.

In helping others through their woundedness, are we not experiencing healing for ourselves? (I believe we do.) In employing our wounds for the benefit of someone else's woundedness, do we not feel better about our own woundedness because of that? (I believe we do.) In giving healing, do we not receive some healing? (I believe we do.)

Who is helping who in the woundedness-to-healing process? Who is not helping? Who is not being helped? Many times I have felt as though I have received from my hospice patients more than I could ever hope to give in return. In helping others, we often find ourselves being helped. The healing process is often a process of mutual healing: everyone involved is being healed, everyone is helping others to heal.

Our attitudes and manifestations of congruence, empathy, and unconditional positive regard facilitate healing. In having and showing congruence, empathy, and unconditional positive regard, we help others to heal and we help ourselves to heal. No matter what our pain, suffering, or imperfections as helpers, counselors, or friends and no matter what the pain, suffering, and imperfections of those who come to us for help, we can receive healing and we can give healing.

The Buddhist Pema Chodron has said, "Our life's work is to use what we have been given to wake up. . . . It doesn't matter what you're given, whether it's physical deformity or enormous wealth or poverty, beauty or ugliness, mental stability or mental instability, life in the middle of a madhouse or life in the middle of a peaceful, silent desert." [4] Coming from the same spiritual tradition as Pema Chodron, Sogyal Rinpoche has said that "there is no situation, however seemingly hopeless or terrible . . . which we cannot use to evolve." [5] That is the challenge that is before each one of us, the challenge of our particular wounds and the wounds of others. That is the challenge of the spiritual model: how will we use our wounds to evolve, how will we use our wounds to heal ourselves and to heal others.

REFLECTION

Bring to mind one of your serious imperfections or shortcomings.

Write down (or verbally share) all the reasons why you feel people would not love you because of that imperfection or shortcoming.

Write down (or verbally share) two or three sentences that can refute each of the "reasons" you stated above.

REFLECTION

Write down (or verbally share) a description of a person who is one of the most wounded persons you know, someone who has experienced more losses than anyone else you know.

Write down (or verbally share) five sentences of positive things this person gives you. Each sentence would begin, "This person gives me . . ."

REFLECTION

Write down (or verbally share) how you would define "congruence" (authenticity) in a caregiver.

Write down (or verbally share) how you would define "empathy" in a caregiver.

Write down (or verbally share) how you would define "unconditional positive regard" in a caregiver.

Chapter Two
References

1. Ram Dass & Gorman, P. (1985). How Can I Help?. New York: Alfred A. Knopf.

2. Rogers, C. R. (1961). On Becoming A Person. Boston: Houghton Mifflin.

3. Hillman, J. (1979). Puer's Wound and Ulysses' Scar. In Puer Papers (pp. 100-128). Dallas: Spring Publications.

4. Pema Chodron. (1991). The Wisdom Of No Escape. Boston: Shambhala.

5. Sogyal Rinpoche. (1992). The Tibetan Book Of Living And Dying. New York: HarperCollins.

Relationships With And Without Dominance

Throughout our lives we witness relationships of dominance: males over females, whites over people of color, the politically powerful over the politically powerless, the economically advantaged over the economically disadvantaged, priest over lay person, doctor over patient, therapist over client. These relationships of dominance are often disguised by the person who is in the dominant role with words like "it is for the common good" and "it is for your own good." However, our experience seems to prove over and over again that relationships of dominance are often not for "the common good," and they are only for "our own good" when we are in the dominant roles. Also, if we really examine relationships of dominance closely, we discover that such relationships are only superficially good for the dominant person; no one really gains through such relationships.

In the field of organized religion, we see over and over again the dominance motif being presented in many forms. Religious leaders remain standing while lay people must sit, kneel, or prostrate themselves. Religious leaders climb pulpits or platforms to further distance themselves. Religious leaders get to wear special clothes that no one else can wear, clothes that can often completely cover the shape of their humanness, making these religious leaders look rather angelic. Religious leaders are addressed by special titles like "father," "pastor," "rabbi," or "master." Religious leaders are often thought of as the unique gatekeepers to that which is holy. I do not believe such a clear relationship of dominance promotes growth or healing. If it did promote growth and healing, there would not be so many people totally rejecting organized religion. If it did promote growth and healing, there would not be so many people permanently scarred emotionally because of organized religion. And is it not true that people are often rejecting organized religion and getting scarred emotionally by it precisely because of that relationship of dominance? Such a relationship of dominance does not even help the person who is in the dominant role in areas of growth and healing — especially when we examine the high rates of alcoholism and mental disorders among clergy (some of the highest rates of any profession). And is it not true that clergy are often having those problems precisely because they cannot emotionally handle their supposed dominance?

In the field of medicine, we also see over and over again the dominance motif being presented in many forms. Patients wear hospital gowns with their back sides exposed. Such defenseless patients are placed before doctors who often have special additional clothing to wear over the clothing they already have. Also, various tools hang around doctors' necks or are placed in their pockets, tools used to probe, poke, and scrutinize the patient's body. Rarely can anyone ever call a doctor by his or her first name. Also, medical professionals are infamous for having people wait for them, communicating to everyone that their time is somehow more valuable than anyone else's time. I do not believe such a clear relationship of dominance promotes growth or healing. If it did promote growth and healing, there would not be so many people frantically running to medicine cabinets and emergency rooms when they get something as simple as a headache or a common cold. People have been so duped by this relationship of dominance that they believe that pills and doctors are the answers to every problem. Such a relationship of dominance does not even help the person who is in the dominant role in areas of growth and healing — especially when we examine the high rates of divorce and drug abuse among physicians (some of the highest rates of any profession). And is it not true that physicians are often having those problems precisely because they cannot emotionally handle their supposed dominance?

In the field of psychotherapy, we also see over and over again the dominance motif being presented in many forms. Here we see the psychological equivalent of physical probing, poking, and scrutinizing. We see psychotherapists often portraying themselves as emotionally untouchable and invulnerable, maintaining a "clinical distance." We see therapists labeling clients as "abnormal," somehow inferior to that which is "standard," classifying these clients as a number on some chart of reimbursement codes. We see clear financial gains for the therapist if he or she encourages the client's dependence. I do not believe such a clear relationship of dominance promotes growth and healing. If it did promote growth and healing, there would not be so many people "stuck" in therapy, "addicted" to therapy. And is it not true that these people are often "stuck" in therapy precisely because of that relationship of dominance? Such a relationship of dominance does not even help the person who is in the dominant role in areas of growth and healing — especially when we examine the high rates of depression and suicide among psychotherapists (some of the highest rates of any profession). And is it not true that psychotherapists are often having those problems precisely because they cannot emotionally handle their supposed dominance?

Relationships of dominance do not promote growth and healing. The dominated do not grow and heal. Those who dominate do not grow and heal.

Much of the explanation for why growth and healing do not take place within the environment of a relationship of dominance is because in such a relationship there can be no congruence, empathy, and unconditional positive regard. Congruence (authenticity) is impossible because congruence assumes an admittance by the helper that he or she is vulnerable, wounded, and imperfect: relationships of dominance hide the dominant person's vulnerability, woundedness, and imperfections. Empathy (experiencing another's woundedness as if it were our own) is also impossible in a relationship of dominance because a relationship of dominance thrives upon creating distance, not closeness, between the dominant one and the person who is dominated. Unconditional positive regard is also impossible for the very same reason: relationships of dominance are based upon the false perception that there are "conditions" that make us unequal. Consequently, there can be little doubt as to why growth and healing would have little chance of occurring within a relationship of dominance, little chance for those being dominated, little chance for those dominating.

Even though we can all easily see how relationships of dominance do not promote growth and healing, we still perpetuate these relationships. For example, many forms of medical and psychological care appear to be evolving toward more and more depersonalization of the patient/client relationship, more and more distancing between the supposed helper and the person seeking help. Within medical and psychological care, we are looking at ever increasing paper work, trying to fit people into forms, interpreting people statistically, defining and comparing them — just another way of subjugating people. With increasing frequency the bywords within medical and psychological care are "measurable outcomes," defining people in terms of statistical data and goals — more and more depersonalization, more and more victimization through dominance.

For those of us in "helping professions," we often foster and preserve these relationships of dominance. We become a parent-like figure and treat our patients or clients as if they are child-like. We take control over the lives of patients and clients; we direct and insist on various changes. Such relationships are not conducive to the healing of others or to our own healing.

There can sometimes be a need for some type of dominant role when modeling or teaching is needed. However, not when growth and healing is needed.

In Lewis Carroll's Through the Looking-Glass, just before she meets Tweedledum and Tweedledee, Alice enters the wood-of-no-names where she meets a fawn. Neither Alice nor the fawn are able to remember their names. In this condition of not knowing each other's names, they wander through the woods together, the fawn snuggling up to Alice, Alice's arms lovingly draped around the fawn's neck. Then the two of them come to the edge of the wood where the fawn suddenly recalls its name and, with horror, looks at Alice. "I'm a Fawn!" it cries out, "and dear me! you're a human child!" Completely terrified, it runs away.

Relationships of dominance need labeling, defining, and comparing in order for the dominance to be maintained; relationships of dominance feed upon labeling, defining, and comparing. As Abraham Maslow has said, "Pathologizing dichotomizes; dichotomizing pathologizes." [1] As K. Louise Schmidt has said, "Binary or dualistic logic sees the world in either/or terms: good or bad, strong or weak. . . . When binary thinking places the differences between people within a paradigm for human relations of supremacy and subordination, the result is alienation and violence." [2] Relationships of dominance produce labeling, defining, and comparing; labeling, defining, and comparing produce relationships of dominance.

If I participate in a relationship of dominance where the other is labeled "the competent one," I become and remain labeled "the incompetent one." If I participate in a relationship of dominance where the other is the holder of power, I become and remain a person without power. If I participate in a relationship of dominance where the other is labeled "the healthy one," I become and remain labeled "the unhealthy one." In such relationships, can the supposed non-competent, powerless, unhealthy person ever grow and experience healing? In such relationships, can the supposed competent, powerful, healthy person ever grow? The answer to both of these questions is obviously "no."

If growth and healing are to ever occur, we need to eliminate these relationships of dominance because these relationships of dominance get in the way of congruence, empathy, and unconditional positive regard, and these relationships are really not good for anybody. If growth and healing are to ever occur, we need to recognize that we are not opposites to one another. I am not all bad and you all good; I am not unhealthy and you healthy; I am not wounded and you whole; we all have some weakness, deficiencies, some unhealthiness: we all have woundedness.

There are two reasons why we, as potential helpers, need to examine our own vulnerability, our imperfections, our pain and suffering, our woundedness. One, people find it much easier to be open with open people; those wishing to be helped find it much easier to be open with an open healer. Two, if we cannot find healing for our own woundedness, we will have great difficulty in helping others find healing for their woundedness.

As mentioned earlier, the sharing of our woundedness must, however, never convey or imply a type of boasting ("I can fully understand your pain because of the pain I have experienced." Or: "You can get through your pain because I have gone through worse."). Also, as mentioned earlier as well, such sharing must not involve completely abdicating the helper role: exploiting the person who has come to us for help, exploiting that person solely for our own benefit. Any bragging about our woundedness or exploiting people to help us when we have been asked to be the helper will definitely not do much in helping ourselves or others.

That being said, we still need to openly explore our woundedness in order to establish our own congruence and find our own healing. In sharing our woundedness with congruence, without boasting or exploiting, we can help ourselves to grow and heal and we can help others to grow and heal.

In hiding our vulnerability and woundedness by fostering a relationship of dominance, we prevent healing, our own healing and the healing of others. In fact, relationships of dominance not only do not lead to healing, they often lead to destruction, the destruction of others and our own destruction. I discovered this fact while being a minister in the Episcopal Church.

After working in several increasingly larger congregations, I eventually found myself at a very wealthy congregation in Arizona where I was the Senior Associate Minister on a staff of six clergy. I had a very nice salary, a beautiful home, and a swimming pool. I had achieved an admirable position.

Although I was not excited about all of what I was asked to do, I became thoroughly absorbed in the power game of priest over lay person, organized religion's version of relationships of dominance. I would put up with what I felt were the barely tolerable necessities of altar guilds, church potlucks, prayer groups, and coffee hours. As long as I could have all of the control and receive all of the attention during Sunday morning worship services, I would put up with the other trappings of the ministry.

On those Sunday mornings, I got to enter a pulpit in

fancy robes and preach a sermon to lawyers, doctors, teachers, business leaders, and many other respected people, and they could not ask questions, could not object to what I was saying, and could not even leave while I was speaking to them. I could present a highly rehearsed picture of myself for about an hour, and almost everyone felt that that hour represented my persona twenty-four hours a day, every day of the week. I was putting on a show; I was presenting a picture of a person who really did not exist. People admired me because I was fooling them with that highly rehearsed show, that show that took advantage of my dominant role. As a result, many women perceived me as being smarter, kinder, and more poised than their husbands or boyfriends. I was even fooling myself as I got absorbed in believing that I was really quite an impressive person, almost godlike.

I then took advantage of all of that manufactured power, taking advantage of my dominance, taking advantage of all of that admiration that people were giving me. I enjoyed the power and I abused the power. I ended up sexually deserting my wife for another woman, a woman who was much more impressed with me than my wife. I ended up emotionally deserting my children for people who seemed to appreciate my time more. I ended up spiritually deserting my calling. I ended up completely deserting myself. I was hardly congruent; my life had become a lie.

I eventually became aware of two different voices within me. One voice, a loud voice, wanted me to protect my role of dominance. The other voice, a quiet but insistent voice, told me who I really was: someone who was really no better than anyone else. I tried to stop the quiet voice, but it kept being insistent; I tried to fully bury that voice, but it would not be buried.

As a result of my inability to settle my internal war of voices, I began manifesting some strange behavior. I would be doing a worship service and suddenly start sweating profusely. I would be talking to someone and suddenly take on a blank stare, needing to be shaken back into consciousness. I would be driving my car and would suddenly discover that I was someplace where I had no intent of going. I would have repeated dreams of being chased and chased.

One morning I awoke to find myself in a mental institution. Wire-mesh was on all of the windows. All of the walls were painted grey.

For the next six weeks, I acclimated myself to a new daily regimen: breakfast pill call, breakfast, unstructured group therapy, free time, lunch pill call, lunch, art and craft therapy, structured group therapy, free time, dinner pill call, dinner, free time, sleep time. During the free time, there might be visits from psychiatrists or visitors from outside the institution. Also, during free time many of the patients were receiving shock treatments.

During my third week there, on a day in which my medication had just been altered, my bishop came to visit me. He came for the sole purpose of having me sign a document entitled "The Renunciation of the Priesthood." I remember crying for hours after he left because this event triggered all the grief I had accumulated related to becoming the person I had become. I cried because I was no longer the person I used to be. I was losing my family, my job, my sanity.

I awoke the next morning to the familiar words of "breakfast pill call." As I awoke, I discovered that I was not alone in my bed. There was a man there, a big man, and he had a knife in his right hand. The knife was held up to his lips indicating that I needed to be silent. Although that man could have done a lot more than masturbate in front of me, as he did, I still felt greatly shamed; I felt a great sense of violation.

That day my resolution to get out of that place became quite intense; I needed to get out of there as soon as possible in order to hold onto whatever sanity I had left. I was determined to do whatever was necessary to get out. I began to stand towards the front of the pill line and would, without any resistance, take my pills. I began to actively participate in the group therapy sessions. I began to make extra efforts in the art and craft classes.

That very next week, the fourth week, I was one of the winners of the weekly Tuesday evening field trip, a special reward for the week's six most well-behaved patients. The six of us were escorted off the hospital grounds by two staff members, loaded into an unmarked, white, windowless van, and driven to a restaurant. In the restaurant parking lot, the six of us had to join hands as one of the staff members led us into the restaurant and the other staff member followed. We were led to a large circular table where we sat down and got to order a dessert from the menu. Upon completing the dessert, we had to hold hands again, be led back to the van, and be driven back to the hospital. I felt so privileged to be chosen for that field trip, not until later realizing how humiliating the whole experience was, not until later realizing that some of my former parishioners could have been in that restaurant.

I did eventually get released from that hospital, although I was released while still on medication and still quite sick. I had no home to go to, no job, no career, no friends, no references; I literally had to begin my life all over again.

I was determined to eventually have a life built upon honesty, built upon an honest realization of my vulnerability, my weaknesses, and my woundedness: trying my hardest to not pretend that I was any greater than anyone else, trying my hardest to have no more relationships of dominance. I had learned how destructive relationships of dominance could be.

I had damaged myself by buying into, and perpetuating, a relationship of dominance. I had pretended to be greater than others and had thereby set myself up to destroy all that I was. I had definitely hurt others, and I had definitely hurt myself. All because I pretended that I was superior to others, pretending to be greater than I really was.

Relationships of dominance do not promote growth and healing. The people dominated do not grow and heal. The people dominating do not grow and heal.

Relationships of dominance can be quite destructive. They can be destructive for the people being dominated. They can be destructive for the people who are dominating.

For growth and healing to take place, there must be congruence, empathy, and unconditional positive regard; there must be the realization that we are all basically alike, all having strengths and weaknesses, all having pain and suffering, all having resources to find growth and healing in the midst of that pain and suffering. Relationships of dominance can be quite destructive and not promote growth and healing because such relationships do not allow for the recognition that we are all basically alike, all having strengths, all having weaknesses.

To get away from these relationships of dominance and to promote growth and healing, we need to deflate the inflated ego and inflate the deflated ego. We need to deflate the egos of religious professionals and inflate the egos of their parishioners. We need to deflate the egos of the medical professionals and inflate the egos of their patients. We need to deflate the egos of psychotherapists and inflate the egos of their clients.

In deflating the inflated ego and in inflating the deflated ego, we come to a place where we can be congruent, real, authentic. We can then truly have empathy for one another. We can then truly have unconditional positive regard for one another. We can then truly receive healing for ourselves and give healing to others.

REFLECTION

Write down (or verbally share) a description of a "relationship of dominance" that you have where you are the dominant one.

Write down (or verbally share) three ways (verbal or behavioral messages that you give) whereby you perpetuate your dominant position.

Write down (or verbally share) how this relationship hinders the growth of those you dominate.

Write down (or verbally share) how this relationship hinders your growth as an individual.

REFLECTION

Read, read again, and meditate upon the following:

"To become more profound, give up your selfishness. Let go of your efforts to be perfect or rich or secure or admired. Such efforts only limit you. They block your universality." [3]

REFLECTION

Read, read again, and meditate upon the following:

"Good behavior is not meant to build us up so that we can think of ourselves as little princes or princesses. The point of good behavior is to communicate our respect for others." [4]

REFLECTION

Read, read again, and meditate upon the following:

"He does not think there is anything the matter with him
because
    one of the things that is
    the matter with him
    is that he does not think that there is anything
    the matter with him
therefore
    we have to help him realize that,
    the fact that he does not think there is anything
    the matter with him
    is one of the things that is
    the matter with him." [5]

REFLECTION

Read, read again, and meditate upon the following:

"Why is the ocean the greatest body of water? Because it lies below all the rivers and streams and is open to them all." [6]

Chapter Three
References

1. Maslow, A. H. (1962). Toward A Psychology Of Being. Princeton, NY: D. Van Nostrand.

2. Schmidt, K. L. (1995). Transforming Abuse. Gabriola Island, BC: New Society Publishers.

3. Heider, J. (1985). The Tao Of Leadership. New York: Bantam Books.

4. Chogyam Trungpa. (1984). Shambhala: The Sacred Path Of The Warrior. Boulder, CO: Shambhala.

5. Laing, R. D. (1970). Knots. New York: Vintage Books.

6. Heider, J. (1985). The Tao Of Leadership. New York: Bantam Books.

Life
With And Without Armor

There is one mistake that we can easily make that keeps us from growth and healing: the mistake of not acknowledging who we really are. In relationships of dominance, we see this mistake: the person in the dominant role is somehow presented as being greater than is actually the case and the dominated one is forced into accepting the message that he or she is less than is actually the case.

A large part of the problem for those of us who are in dominant roles (no matter what the relationship) is in failing to acknowledge our own woundedness. We feel we should try to hide or escape from anything that shows our vulnerability, and that if we could just learn how to do that, we would be happy. We sometimes feel as though the secret to life has to somehow involve assertiveness training and the power of positive thinking: if we just think of ourselves as being stronger than what we are, we will be stronger. We feel that to get something we do not have, we have to merely pretend to be someone we are not. Ironically, in reality, our desire to hide or ignore our own woundedness is oftentimes the very thing that keeps us from growth and healing; our desires to be happy and our attempts at making ourselves happy are oftentimes the very things that keep us unhappy; our emotional "armor," rather than equipping us to forge ahead, actually results in emotional retreat, emotional regression rather than emotional progression.

When someone who wants to be a helper puts on armor (a supposed protective barrier designed to give the appearance of invulnerability), the effectiveness of the helping process is seriously jeopardized. As Carl Jung has said, "The patient . . . can win his own inner security only from the security of his relationship to the [helper] as a human being. The [helper] can put over his authority with fairly good results on people who are easily gulled. But for critical eyes it is apt to look a little too threadbare. . . . It is his own hurt that gives the measure of his power to heal." [1] For the helping process to be effective, we, as helpers, need to let go of our armor, no matter what form that armor takes: overemphasizing our authority, our knowledge, our degrees, our titles, or our strength. In the letting go of that armor, growth and healing become possible, for ourselves and for others.

If we cannot accurately perceive ourselves, how can we perceive anyone else accurately? If we have false perceptions of ourselves, how can we have true perceptions of others? How can we persuade someone to lead an authentic life if we do not lead one? We must first be willing to look at ourselves accurately; we must first be willing to acknowledge our own shortcomings, weaknesses, and vulnerability; we must get beyond our own false perceptions of ourselves and let go of our armor.

In admitting our own shortcomings and loving ourselves in spite of those shortcomings, we can help others admit their own shortcomings, helping them to love themselves in spite of those shortcomings (a true expression of healing). In admitting our own weaknesses and loving ourselves in spite of those weaknesses, we can help others admit their own weaknesses, helping them to love themselves in spite of those weaknesses (a true expression of healing). In admitting our own vulnerability and loving ourselves in spite of that vulnerability, we can help others admit their own vulnerability, helping them to love themselves in spite of their vulnerability (a true expression of healing). If we ignore our own shortcomings, weaknesses, and vulnerability, how can we ever hope to help others with their shortcomings, weaknesses, and vulnerability? How dare we even address the woundedness of others if we have not addressed our own woundedness.

The medical model often used by modern medicine and modern psychology emphasizes changes and cures so strongly that people end up ignoring their natural state of always having wounds; the medical model can often dupe people into believing in some impossible ideal that is always out of reach, the impossible ideal that our state of woundedness can be eliminated. Sometimes people can be falsely persuaded into believing that they can somehow go through life and avoid wounds. That is not a helpful message for anyone. It is nice to offer and provide changes and cures for various ailments, but various changes and cures for various ailments must be seen for what they are: treatments for very limited portions of very complex and very fragile human beings — hardly harbingers of the possibility of a society without wounds.

The spiritual model that I am presenting, on the

other hand, does not offer such false promises. The spiritual model advocates for the acceptance of shortcomings, weaknesses, and vulnerability: accepting and loving ourselves with our shortcomings, weaknesses, and vulnerability, and accepting and loving others with their shortcomings, weaknesses, and vulnerability. What is being called for is not a defeatist attitude or a belittling attitude, but a realistic one — the realistic attitude of knowing that we cannot eliminate all woundedness. However, even though we cannot eliminate all woundedness, we can learn to live with our own woundedness, love ourselves in spite of that woundedness, love others with their wounds, experience some healing for ourselves, and help others find some healing for themselves.

Men will often have an especially challenging job in the open and honest admittance of their shortcomings, weaknesses, and vulnerability. We often need to work hard to get in touch with our physical and psychological armor and the many forms that armor can take. We often need to work hard to learn about how much our various forms of armor hide the many dimensions of our total selves, learning about how much that armor hinders us in doing some real healing, hindering us in becoming complete, well-rounded, healthy individuals.

In calling for the withdrawal from being dominant and in calling for the letting go of armor to get in touch with our woundedness, I am calling for congruence, the first condition for growth (the first quality that the would-be helper must establish for the easy facilitation of healing). We must get rid of that which covers up our true selves.

Once we have let go of our armor and our need to be dominant, establishing our congruence, we can then go on to having empathy. In having empathy, the second condition for growth/healing, we are feeling the other's feelings, being concerned about the other's concerns. In having empathy, we feel for the other person and with the other person, something we cannot do until we first become congruent.

After becoming congruent (letting go of our armor and our need to be dominant), and after establishing our empathy, we can then go on to having unconditional positive regard. In having unconditional positive regard for the other, the third condition for growth/healing, we are saying that we must not just value the other's feelings and concerns, we must also value the other, the person who has those feelings and concerns, valuing that person unconditionally. We respect and value the other, even if the other is different from us in thinking or lifestyle, even if the other is not congruent, even if the other does not have empathy for us, even if the other is not even close to having unconditional positive regard for us.

Of course, armor is not always "bad" or "wrong." People sometimes need armor. Some situations require armor. However, if we wish to grow and heal as individuals, we must keep our armor at a minimum. And, if we wish to facilitate growth and healing in another, we must also have our armor at a minimum. In minimizing that armor, we begin to establish our own congruence, empathy, and unconditional positive regard. We thus facilitate our own healing and the healing of others.

In hospice work, I have often seen people taking off their armor and witnessed the healing that comes to these people as they do that. The dying process many times even forces people into taking off their armor. The following dialogue illustrates the kind of healing that results from such loss of armor.

Tom was a gruff, highly controlled individual who was dying of prostate cancer. One day I was in his room with his wife and sister when the following occurred:

Tom: "I want everyone to leave the room except for Doug. I would like the women to leave."

The women left the room. Tom then searched my face as if he were trying to see if he could trust me.

Tom: "I got a problem."

Doug: "What?"

Tom: "I can't cry!"

Doug: "What?"

Tom (practically shouting): "I can't cry, dammit!"

Doug: "And you want to cry?"

Tom: "Yeah. I want to cry."

Doug: "What's holding you back, Tom?"

Tom: "I don't know how."

Doug: "You don't know how?"

Tom (practically shouting): "Yeah. I don't know how!"

Doug: "Why do you have to know how?"

Tom (practically shouting): "Because, you can't do anything you don't know how to do! What are you, dense?"

Doug: "Let's just calm down, Tom. Calm down. . (He calmed down a little.) . . . You sound angry."

Tom (Immediately stiffening up again, he shouts.): "I am angry, dammit! I can't cry!"

Doug: "Tom, tears are usually because of sadness, not anger. . . . Are you sad?"

Tom (after a long pause): "Yeah, dammit! I'm sad!"

Doug: "Tom, hug me."

Tom: "What?"

Doug: "You heard me. Hug me."

Tom: "I'm not going to hug you!"

Doug: "Tom, hug me."

Tom: "No!"

Doug: "Tom, put your arms around me and hug me."

Tom: "Why?"

Doug: "Tom, put your arms around me and hug me."

Tom (Edging a little closer, he seemed a little calmer.): "How's that going to help?"

Doug: "Tom, put your arms around me and hug me."

He wrapped his arms around me. They felt like two baseball bats attached to a robot.

Tom (talking through his teeth): "Now what?"

Doug: "Relax."

He tightened up some more.

Doug: "Relax."

He was silent. He loosened up a little.

Doug: "Relax some more, Tom."

His baseball bats were getting softer; the robot appeared to be getting deprogrammed. He was silent.

Doug: "Relax some more, Tom."

His arms were now softly enfolded around me.

Doug: "Relax, Tom. . . . It's okay. It's okay to let go. It's okay to cry."

There was a still silence, a little tightening, then a little more loosening, then a faint quiver throughout his entire body, then the quiver started building, starting to become a shake, then he swallowed loudly two times, then a soft choking sound, then he started bawling, gushing tears, and more tears, and more tears.

After thoroughly soaking my shirt with tears, Tom unwrapped his arms and stood back. He stood back with a softness, a softness I had never before seen on him.

Tom: "That felt good, real good. You don't know how good that felt. . . . It felt real good! Dammit! That felt real good!"

I believe that some growth and healing took place there. That growth and healing took place primarily because Tom allowed himself to let go of some armor. He was also assisted in that process through his terminal illness, and, in a small way, through my willingness to let him cry. Tom let go of his need to be in control, let go of his armor, saw his woundedness, accepted his woundedness, and then somehow experienced some growth and healing through the acceptance of that woundedness.

The goal of Buddhism can be easily understood as not striving for perfection but rather seeing ourselves as we really are, apart from our armor. Practicing Buddhism means accepting our natural state with all its imperfections, seeing ourselves as we really are, having mindfulness for what actually is: that's the goal of Buddhism. The name "Buddha" essentially means "being awake to what actually is," imperfections and all.

The goal of Christianity can also be easily understood as not striving for perfection but rather seeing ourselves as we really are, apart from our armor. Practicing Christianity means accepting our natural state of brokenness and realizing that our own salvation comes through the realistic confession of that brokenness. The name "Jesus" essentially means "God is with us," brokenness and all, imperfections and all.

Our armor, rather than protecting us, actually hinders us, hindering us from fully centering upon reality as it is, with all the woundedness and all the wonderfulness. That is what the spiritual model says.

Although this message seems very strange to much of our modern consciousness, it still proves itself true experientially. Oftentimes, when I am aware that I am the most lost, that is when I am about ready to find something truly great. Oftentimes, when I am aware that I am the most lonely, that is when I am about ready to experience a presence that is truly profound. Oftentimes, when I am aware that I am the most distraught, that is when I am about ready to be given the most comforting of messages. Dean Ornish, apparently having similar experiences, has said that "during the times that we feel most vulnerable, that which is invulnerable within us becomes uncovered, becomes more apparent." [2]

Those seeking help want their helpers to be both knowledgeable and humble, professional and human. If people just want knowledge to address their woundedness, they will choose a book or an audiotape for their therapy. If people want special knowledge authenticated by special degrees and titles, they will choose a book or an audiotape by someone with impressive degrees and credentials. However, when they choose a person, a human being, as opposed to a book or an audiotape, that is what they want:

a person, a human being, humble, vulnerable, real, a fellow wounded traveller.

When we as helpers drop our armor, allowing our woundedness to surface, we allow for healing in ourselves and healing in others. When we all meet in that place where there is no armor, growth and healing do indeed become possible, even probable.

After I had been moved out of hospice patient care into hospice administrative work, I made it known to the entire staff that if there was ever a situation where I could help in patient care, when no patient care staff was available, I would be glad to help, no matter how seemingly “menial” the situation might be. At the time, I did not realize all the possible scenarios that could arise if people took me seriously, of which they did. Somehow I did not expect that I would be called upon to give a man a bath or remove a catheter from a dead woman’s body, activities which I was called upon to do soon after I had made that invitation, activities which I was ill-prepared to do given my training as a counselor, a spiritual care provider, and a health care administrator.

One day, our receptionist buzzed me in my office saying that a patient named Gary needed some immediate assistance from a home health aide and there were no home health aides available. Gary, who had ALS, was at home alone and had just had diarrhea and was unable to clean himself. The receptionist asked if I could drive over to Gary's house and clean him. My offer to assist in patient care was once again being taken seriously.

When I arrived at Gary's house, I let myself in, and immediately started to clean Gary with little difficulty. Why was I able to clean him with little difficulty? How could I clean him with hardly a second thought? I could do that because of Gary's woundedness and his letting go of armor. As difficult as it was for me to get rid of my own armor of "administrative respectability" and wipe the diarrhea off Gary's body, I realized I could easily do that because Gary was being faced with having to get rid of much more serious armor than I; as difficult as it is to clean diarrhea off someone, it is much more difficult to have to ask someone to clean diarrhea off of you. Because Gary was first willing to do the more difficult task of taking off his serious armor of "dignity" to ask me to clean him, I could easily take off my silly armor of "administrative respectability."

That day I grew as a person. I grew because I learned more about congruence, empathy, and unconditional positive regard. I grew because Gary was willing to take off his armor, and, consequently, he helped me take off my armor. He helped me experience some healing.

By letting go of our armor, we can grow, we can

become "stronger" in the real sense of that word. By dying to our old self, we can live with a new self, a better self. By giving, we receive, receiving something of greater value than what we give.

We can see this truth in the realm of our intellectual lives. The more we use our minds, the greater our minds become; the more we expend from our minds, the more our minds receive. If we try to save or preserve our minds by not reading and not studying and not thinking, look what happens: our minds do not grow, but become dull and die. If we "protect" our minds, if we shield our minds with armor, our minds disappear. How ridiculous it is to try to save and preserve our minds by not expending them, by "protecting" them. How absurd it is to think that we can retain our minds by not exercising them, by keeping them away from any interaction. If we try to keep our minds to ourselves and never open them up to anyone or anything else, we literally "lose our minds." It is only in the giving of our minds that we receive for our minds; it is only in the taking down of the armor around our minds that our minds begin to grow.

We can see this truth in the realm of our physical lives as well. The more we exercise our muscles, the stronger our muscles become. If we try to save and preserve our muscles by not exercising and not working, we know what happens to our muscles: our muscles do not gain strength, but become flaccid and useless. If we "protect" our muscles, if we keep them away from any interaction, muscle tissue literally disappears. Reality teaches us that if we do not use our muscles now, we will not have them later. If our muscles are to ever gain anything, they must first give and serve. Our physical body can never experience growth without first learning how to humble itself through expending itself, not by "protecting" itself.

Does it not make sense that that which is true for our intellectual lives and our physical lives might also have some validity for our psychological, emotional, and spiritual lives? There are certain moments in our lives, in the lives of everyone, in which we are forced into psychological, emotional, and spiritual humility, when we are forced into letting go of all of our psychological, emotional, and spiritual armor, when we are forced into expending ourselves psychologically, emotionally, and spiritually. At those moments, we are usually on the brink of some profound growth, some profound healing.

In the giving of our psychological, emotional, and spiritual energy, we grow psychologically, emotionally, and spiritually. And even when we get to those places that sometimes feel like the most vulnerable places we have ever been, we discover that that "bottom" can sometimes be a takeoff point for some marvelous growth and healing, healing that comes through letting go, letting go of our armor.

REFLECTION

Write down (or verbally share) five advantages that people might receive by having armor.

Write down (or verbally share) five disadvantages that people might receive through that armor.

REFLECTION

Write down (or verbally share) two weaknesses that you feel you have which hinder you from being a better person than you are.

Write down (or verbally share) tactics that you use to try to cover up these weaknesses so that they are not evident to those around you.

Write down (or verbally share) what you feel would be the worst thing that could happen to you if everyone knew about these weaknesses.

Write down (or verbally share) what you feel you might possibly gain if everyone knew about your weaknesses.

REFLECTION

Write down (or verbally share) about a time in your life when you grew as a result of letting go of some armor that you had.

REFLECTION

Read, read again, and meditate upon the following:

"Egoism is like trying to swim without relying on the water, endeavoring to keep afloat by tugging at your own legs; your whole body becomes tense, and you sink like a stone. Swimming requires a certain relaxation, a certain giving of yourself to the water." [3]

REFLECTION

Read, read again, and meditate upon the following:

"Sometimes we worry about losing what we have gained. We think of ourselves as already 'there,' and we resist anything new. But if we don't have anything to hang onto and protect, then we receive much more readily." [4]

Chapter Four
References

1. Jung, C. G. (1954). The Practice Of Psychotherapy (R. F. C. Hull, Trans.). Princeton, NJ: Princeton University Press.

2. Ornish, D. (1996). Forward. In R. N. Remen, Kitchen Table Wisdom. New York: Riverhead Books.

3. Watts, A. (1947). Behold The Spirit. New York: Vintage Books.

4. Huang, A. (1973). Embrace Tiger, Return To Mountain. Moab, UT: Real People Press.

Humility Training Or Assertiveness Training

For those of us that find ourselves in the role of being the dominant one in a relationship of dominance, there is most likely a need for us to have some humility training so that we might portray a more accurate picture of our true selves. For those of us that find ourselves as the dominated one in a relationship of dominance, there is most likely some need for us to have some assertiveness training in order to portray a more accurate picture of our true selves. When we find ourselves in the midst of relationships of dominance, we often need to deflate the inflated ego and inflate the deflated ego.

Those of us in dominant positions need to deflate our egos; we need to have some humility training. This need for humility training, this need for acknowledging our woundedness, is talked about throughout the literature of our major spiritual traditions. Taoist literature says, "Let yourself be empty." [1] Hindu scripture says, "The man who claims that he knows, knows nothing; but he who claims nothing, knows." [2] Within the Buddhist tradition, we read, "What looks like weakness is actually where your strength lies. And what looks like strength is often weakness." [3] Jewish scripture says, "Humility precedes honor." [4] Christian scripture says, "He who exalts himself shall be humbled and he who humbles himself shall be exalted." [5] Within the Muslim tradition, we read, "Unfathom yourself if you can. If you find out your own limits, it will be the takeoff point to the limitless." [6]

However, even with all of that support from our spiritual traditions, we who occupy dominant roles normally champion an aggressive assertiveness, seriously doubting any benefits to exercising any form of humility. We would normally want to hold onto relationships of dominance if we are the dominant ones. If we are the dominant ones, we normally want to hide our suffering, even to the point of denying it; we normally want to hide our woundedness, even to the point of denying that we have any woundedness.

We, the dominant ones, normally think that if we act strong, hiding our woundedness, we will be productive, attain respect, and be "healthy, wealthy, and wise." Yet, do we ever really thoroughly examine the truth of such a belief? Can we, or anyone, really "respect" someone who we know is hiding something from us? Is hiding, or ignoring, several aspects of ourselves really a "healthy" thing to do? Is that hiding of parts of ourselves really a sign of "wisdom"? Can we really feel good about any "wealth" that we might attain from not being true to ourselves?

Although assertiveness training is not right for those that dominate because it further inflates the ego of someone whose ego is already too inflated, it is certainly appropriate for those that are dominated — counteracting the message that they are somehow inferior to others. Yet, the goal of such assertiveness training for the dominated is not to get those that are dominated to become those that dominate. The goal is to get all of us at the same level, where we are all helpers and all in need of help, the place of our shared humanity, the place of our mutual wounds and mutual strengths.

We need to deflate the inflated ego and inflate the deflated ego. Those of us who are religious professionals often need to have our egos lowered through humility training to get to our true identities; our congregants need to have their egos raised to get to their true identities. Those of us who are medical professionals often need to have our egos lowered through humility training to get to our true identities; our patients need to have their egos raised to get to their true identities. Those of us who are psychological professionals often need to have our egos lowered through humility training to get to our true identities; our clients need to have their egos raised to get to their true identities. We, as helpers, often need to deflate our own egos while we inflate the egos of those we wish to help.

We, as professional helpers, often need to deflate our own egos if we are to be honest, authentic, congruent. We often need to deflate our own egos if we are to be empathic. We often need to deflate our own egos if we are to show unconditional positive regard. We often need to deflate our own egos if we are to give and receive healing.

Our lives are filled with reminders of our need to be humble. Our spouse might be such a reminder. Our children can be reminders. Our jobs. Our bodies. We can have many reminders — gifts to make us humble, gifts to keep us humble, gifts to make us congruent, gifts to keep us congruent.

One of my own reminders comes from my body: a problem I have shared with my mother and my grandmother. It is a problem that reminds me of my need to be humble. It is my shaking problem, my gift to make and keep me humble.

My mother once spent a great amount of money to go to the Mayo Clinic to have her shaking problem diagnosed. After numerous tests with consultation from several specialists, my mother was informed that she, my grandmother, and I had something that the doctors at the Mayo Clinic diagnosed as "familial tremor" (a fancy way of saying "family shakes"). Whether I am giving a talk in front of a couple hundred people or at home alone, I can shake — a mild tremor that is most evident in my hands.

I have put myself through all sorts of ridiculous gymnastics in order to not have that problem discovered by others. Whenever someone I have never met asks me if I would like to have a cup of coffee, I have almost always had to say, "No thank you." Whenever I have been eating a business lunch, I have tried to wait until people are looking some other direction than my direction before I take a sip of my beverage. Also, there are several things I try to never order when I am eating in public: soup or peas or anything else that is likely to fall off my spoon or fork. All of this behavior is done in an effort to hide my woundedness so as to protect my "respectability" and "authority," trying to protect some image that I want others to have of me.

Probably my most embarrassing moment happened when I was officiating at a worship service when I was in the ministry: an Ash Wednesday service. As it came time for me to distribute the ashes on people's foreheads, I discovered that the altar guild had forgotten to mix oil with the ashes. That oil was a very important ingredient for the mutual convenience of ministers and parishioners; the oil was needed to form the ashes into a thick paste so that the ashes would stick to the minister's thumb and then easily transfer to the parishioners' foreheads, where the ashes would remain until scrubbed off at the end of the day. Forgetting the oil meant that the ashes would neither stick to a minister's thumb nor to a parishioner's forehead. Adding my shakes to the equation meant that absolutely anything could happen. Practically everything imaginable did happen.

As I made my way around the communion rail on that particular Ash Wednesday, my clerical robe gathered more and more spilt ashes on the sleeves as well as on the outer fringes of the robe's bottom. Little piles of ashes were also accumulating around the inside of the altar rail as I proceeded to carefully step over each little pile. (I was uncertain as to why I was stepping so carefully, not knowing what the theological significance might be to me stepping on the spilt ashes.)

After the parishioners received ashes at the altar rail, they stood and turned around to face the congregation before proceeding to their pews. The parishioners waiting in line to come forward closely witnessed men with ashes on their noses and ties as well as women with ashes on their eyebrows and dresses — even a few cleavages were adorned with ashes. I pitied the devout parishioners who would wear those ashes the entire day no matter where they might have landed.

My shakes are a gift, a gift to remind me to be humble. We need such reminders to keep us from overinflating our egos, to keep us congruent, to keep us able to express empathy and unconditional positive regard.

Our true power, strength, and effectiveness come as the result of accepting ourselves as people possessing brokenness and vulnerability. Yet, this is so contrary to what we "imagine" our power, strength, and effectiveness to be. What we imagine our power, strength, and effectiveness to be is a sham, so much of a sham that everyone sees the sham clearly for what it is: a pretending to be somebody we are not, perhaps even a terrible fear of facing who we really are.

Only in the facing of who we really are in all of our vulnerability can we ever open ourselves up to growth and healing. This is what the Jewish spiritual tradition means when it portrays God as saying, "I . . . turn sages back and make nonsense of their knowledge." [7] This is what the Christian spiritual tradition means when it says that God is hiding "things from the wise and intelligent" and revealing "them to babes." [8] This is what the Buddhist spiritual tradition means when it says that "in the beginner's mind there are many possibilities, in the expert's mind there are few." [9] True power, strength, and effectiveness come from a humble acceptance of our woundedness. True power, strength, and effectiveness do not come from pretending that we are invulnerable, but from admitting that we are vulnerable.

Words from the Tao Te Ching:

"If you want to become whole,
let yourself be partial.
If you want to become straight,
let yourself be crooked.
If you want to become full,
let yourself be empty.
If you want to be reborn,
let yourself die.
If you want to be given everything,
give everything up." [10]

As we, those who normally over-assert ourselves, learn humility training, we discover how important it is to not dominate. We discover how important it is to not force our agendas. We discover the importance of our incompleteness. We discover the importance of giving everything up: it is the foundation for true power, strength, and effectiveness.

There is a Buddhist parable about a great spiritual teacher who was one day approached by a university professor wanting to acquire knowledge. The university professor introduced himself by telling the spiritual teacher about all his degrees, publications, and various accomplishments. As the spiritual teacher was pouring his visitor some tea, the tea began to flow all over the sides of the cup onto the professor. Alarmed, the professor declared, "It is overflowing! No more can go in!" To which the spiritual teacher responded, "Like this cup of tea, you are also full, too full of your own self-importance. How can I teach you anything until you first empty your cup?" Thus, through humility training, through "emptying our cup," we grow, learning more about ourselves, more about others, and more about our environment. By "emptying our cup," we become congruent, we can have empathy, and we can show unconditional positive regard. By "emptying our cup," we can heal and be healed. [11]

What is being called for here is a deflation of our sense of self-importance, something called for in all of the major spiritual and religious traditions; Hindu, Buddhist, Jewish, Christian, and Muslim traditions all contain messages against inflating our self-importance. Through those traditions, we are called upon to decrease our sense of separateness, our individuality, and increase our sense of togetherness, our mutuality. According to these traditions, the more of a sense of individuality that we have as dominant ones, the "smaller" we become; the more of a sense of mutuality that we have, the "larger" we become.

The reason we become "larger" when we suppress our false self-importance is because we then have "room" for another. As with the parable of the professor and the cup of tea, we do not have room for anything or anyone when we are "full" of ourselves. However, if we "empty" ourselves of any false sense of self-importance, by taking on humility rather than assertiveness, we become open to receiving others. Then, with an inflation of the egos of those that are dominated and a deflation of the egos of those that dominate, we will meet together in the place of our shared condition of woundedness, a place where healing can occur, for others and for ourselves.

REFLECTION

Spend an entire day trying to make yourself satisfied and/or happy.

On the following day, spend just an hour trying to make someone else satisfied and/or happy.

Write down (or verbally share) about the quantity and quality of "satisfaction" and "happiness" you felt each day.

Write down (or verbally share) about any "growth" or "healing" you might have experienced during each day.

REFLECTION

Read, read again, and meditate upon the following:

"When I am most deeply aware of my fallen nature I am not at all doubting and disbelieving, demonically possessed, in hopeless despair, tragically unhappy, morbidly diseased, flagrantly in error, or wallowing in sin and guilt. On the contrary, . . . I am closer to heaven and hope and truth and happiness and a sound and healthy mind and spirit than ever in my life." [12]

REFLECTION

Read, read again, and meditate upon the following:

"Seek not the Attainment of Perfection, but the Acceptance of Imperfection." [13]

REFLECTION

Read, read again, and meditate upon the following:

"There's a story about an old grandfather clock which had stood in the same corner of the same house for three generations, never stopping in its task of marking the minutes, the hours, and the days. All of its strength and energy came from a heavy weight which was held by a double chain. 'Too bad,' thought its present owner, 'that such an old clock should have to always carry that heavy load.' So he took the weight off the double chain and removed it from the clock. 'Now, why did you do that?' asked the old grandfather clock. 'I thought I ought to make your burden easier,' said the man. 'Please,' said the clock, 'put my weight back. I can do nothing without that burden. I am as good as dead if I cannot carry that load.'" [14]

REFLECTION

Read, read again, and meditate upon the following:

"Our true nature is not some ideal that we have to live up to. It's who we are right now, and that's what we can make friends with and celebrate." [15]

REFLECTION

Read, read again, and meditate upon the following:

"To whatever extent we focus our longing on getting our own way, on doing in order to achieve results, on holding on to things beyond our control, to that extent we are trapped in needless suffering." [16]

REFLECTION

Read, read again, and meditate upon the following:

"We are, all of us, ordinary people. Liberation begins when we know that." [17]

Chapter Five
References

1. Tao Te Ching. (1988). (S. Mitchell, Trans.). New York: HarperCollins.

2. The Ten Principal Upanishads. (1937). (W. B. Yeats and Shree Purohit Swami, Trans.). New York: Collier Books.

3. Kabat-Zinn, J. (1994). Wherever You Go, There You Are. New York: Hyperion.

4. Proverbs 15:33, Tanakh. Philadelphia: The Jewish Publication Society.

5. Luke 18:14, New American Standard Bible.

6. Massud Farzan. (1974). The Tale Of The Reed Pipe. New York: E. P. Dutton.

7. Isaiah 44:25, Tanakh. Philadelphia: The Jewish Publication Society.

8. Matthew 11:25, New American Standard Bible.

9. Suzuki, S. (1970). Zen Mind, Beginner's Mind. (T. Dixon, Ed.). New York: Weatherhill.

10. Tao Te Ching. (1988). (S. Mitchell, Trans.). New York: HarperCollins.

11. Reps, P. (1957). Zen Flesh, Zen Bones. Garden City, NY: Doubleday.

12. Hong, E. (1979). The Downward Ascent. Minneapolis: Augsburg Publishing.

13. Kopp, S. (1977). Back To One. Palo Alto, CA: Science and Behavior Books.

14. Hamilton, J. W. (1965). Serendipity. Westwood, NJ: Fleming H. Revell.

15. Pema Chodron. (1991). The Wisdom Of No Escape. Boston: Shambhala.

16. Kopp, S. (1977). Back To One. Palo Alto, CA: Science and Behavior Books.

17. Singh, K. D. (1998). The Grace In Dying. New York: HarperCollins.

Mutuality

For those of us who are trying to be helpers, it is purely accidental that we are in the helping role and the people in front of us are those seeking help, purely accidental; our places could easily be reversed. There is a thin dividing line between the supposedly healthy and the supposedly sick. We need to realize, as Barbara Deming has realized, that "our own pulse beats in every stranger's throat." [1]

The more we think of ourselves as different from one another, the more differences we end up creating. The more we think of ourselves as "helpers," the more pressure there is on others to be the "helped." The more we think of ourselves as "saviors," the more people feel coerced into feeling that they need to be "saved." Also, as we assert ourselves over others, we encourage things we know are detrimental to growth and healing: separateness, dependency, impotency.

With such asserting of ourselves, we can never experience empathy. How can we ever be "empathic" towards any person we have labeled as different from us without contradicting the very definition of the word "empathy"?

What makes empathy even possible is the

realization that we are all basically alike — there is very little, if any, differences between us. Whatever differences we might have between us, the dividing line between those differences is very thin. The basis of empathy (the second condition for growth) is this realization that we are all made of the same stuff, some strong stuff and some weak stuff, some healthy stuff and some unhealthy stuff, some smart stuff and some not-so-smart stuff, some stuff we like and some stuff we do not like.

Upon entering seminary to study for the ministry, I remember a professor saying something to all of us first year seminarians. He said, "Contrary to what you might think, you have come to seminary not to be ministers, but to be ministered unto. You came here not for the needs of others, but for your own needs." I have come to believe that this professor was saying something quite profound.

Do those of us who go into psychological professions go into those professions to bring comfort to the minds of others or to bring comfort to our own minds? (Probably a little of both.) Do those of us who go into medical professions go into those professions for the well-being of others or for our own well-being? (Probably a little of both.) Do those of us who go into teaching go into that profession to satisfy the thirst for learning we see in others or for our own thirst for learning? (Probably a little of both.) As Sheila Cassidy has said, "The world is not divided into the strong who care and the weak who are cared for. We must each in turn care and be cared for." [2] Karen Wegela concurred in saying, "We are all helpers as well as people who need help." [3]

When we professionals become trapped in labeling supposed differences between people, we become more and more alienated from one another. Priest and parishioner become more and more distant from one another. Therapist and client become more and more out of touch with one another. So, Ram Dass and Paul Gorman have said, "What otherwise could be a profound and intimate relationship becomes ships passing in the night. In the effort to express compassion, we end up feeling estranged. It's distressing and puzzling." [4]

On the other hand, if we do not pay attention to the inventing and labeling of differences, and pay more attention to having empathy, we will enter the arena of our mutual healing. When we share our wounds, we can share our healing.

We might pretend that there are great differences between us. However, when we honestly examine ourselves and others, we realize how much we are interrelated to one another and inseparably tied to one another. When some people are sick, we all share in the sickness. When people die, they take a part of us with them and we take a part of them with us.

Frank and Mildred, ages ninety-one and eighty-nine, had been married for seventy years. They had had no children other than a stillborn child born in 1923. They had named that stillborn child "Sarah."

Frank and Mildred were still living together in their own home when Frank became very ill and had to be admitted to our hospice program. Mildred was determined that she would take care of Frank for as long as she could. However, that resolve soon became very difficult; the demanding tasks of taking care of someone who is dying were too much for an eighty-nine year old.

Even though the caregiving became nearly impossible, Mildred, after seventy years of living with Frank, was not willing to have Frank spend his final days apart from her; she would not have him go to a nursing home and she would not have him go to a hospital. In realizing that Frank had only about a couple more weeks of life, our hospice staff offered a possible answer to Mildred's dilemma. We asked Mildred if she and Frank would like to move in together into a room at our hospice house. They welcomed that opportunity.

Frank and Mildred lived together in that house for sixteen days: Mildred often sleeping in a lounge chair while Frank was asleep in a bed. I remember several times peeking into the room, seeing them peacefully sleeping in the comfort of each other's presence.

One morning, at 5:30 a.m., a nurse was making her

rounds when she looked into Frank and Mildred's room. She saw Mildred lying in the bed with Frank. She walked over towards them. She saw that Mildred was awake, holding Frank's hand, watching the sun come up outside the window. The nurse also saw that Frank was not breathing.

Mildred turned to the nurse and said, "Frank asked me to join him in bed. He then asked me if it was okay for him to leave me and go be with our daughter, Sarah. I said it was okay, but I miss him already." Mildred then turned back towards the window.

We certainly can get close to people we have been with for seventy years. However, we can also get close to people we have known for only a short time: people can get very close to a stillborn child.

Everyone who enters our life becomes a part of us and we become a part of each of them. We are all of the same stuff; we are interrelated; we are inseparable. We experience mutuality all the time.

It is this sense of mutuality, togetherness, that empowers the best of helping relationships. It is this sense of "us," not "me" and "you," which allows for the possibilities of empathy and unconditional positive regard. Through congruence, empathy, and unconditional positive regard we are united in a relationship without dominance, a relationship with as little armor as possible, a relationship with the right balance of humility training and assertiveness training, a relationship of mutuality.

The inventing of differences and the artificial labeling of them perpetuates living without healing; the realization that we have little, if any, differences allows for healing. This is confirmed in the major spiritual traditions where "separation," "alienation," and "estrangement" are frequent descriptions for lesser states of being, whereas "unity," "wholeness," and "atonement" (at-one-ment) are frequent descriptions for greater states of being. Through these traditions we learn that when we are cut off from one another we are also cut off from our transcendental nature, not only separated from one another but also separated from our True Self, our Creator, our Redeemer, Allah, the Tao, enlightenment, salvation.

The medical model has an emphasis on separate people filling separate roles. There is the person who needs a cure and the person who can provide that cure. There is the person who is operated upon and the person who does the operation. There is the person who needs to recover and the person who allows for that recovery to occur. There is separation, separate roles and separate functions.

The spiritual model, on the other hand, has an emphasis on a process characterized by mutuality. The spiritual model says that we are all in need of healing and we all help one another heal. The spiritual model emphasizes how we are all linked to one another and that our linking creates a combined power that is greater than the sum of the individual powers. Christianity says that whenever two or more are gathered in God's name, God is in the midst of them. Buddhism says that the power of the community, the Sangha, is equal to the power of the Buddha. Taoism says that whenever two seeming opposites come together, there is the Tao. The spiritual model says that in overcoming our separation, in discovering our mutuality, we find healing, our True Self, our Creator, our Redeemer, Allah, the Tao, enlightenment, salvation.

One day, while I was a patient in the mental hospital, I found myself approaching a man named Chico. He was in the large common area in a corner of the room, seated on the floor, rocking back and forth, and gazing steadily up at the ceiling. Chico was often in that corner of that room, often rocking back and forth as he was looking up at the ceiling. His posture reminded me of someone in prayer.

Chico was almost always alone, and I was always under the assumption that he preferred being alone; I had never seen or heard him speaking to anyone. One day, I went up beside him, sat down on the floor about six feet away, facing the side of his body, watching him rock back and forth, back and forth.

In watching him from that position (the side view),

I soon became quite dizzy (my medication could have been partially responsible). To end the dizziness, I turned to face the same direction as Chico and began rocking back and forth with him, matching his pace, and periodically glancing over at him. When I was first looking over at him from the sideways position, he was not paying any attention to me. However, when I was facing the same direction that he was, he began to take periodic glançes over at me.

At one moment, we simultaneously glanced at each other, both of us exchanged a quick smile, and then Chico returned to his position and began picking up the pace of rocking back and forth. I quickly matched his pace. We got faster and faster, rocking back and forth, gazing up at the ceiling. Faster and faster. Then Chico suddenly stopped, scooted over next to me so that we were touching one another, wrapped his arm around my shoulder, and began rocking back and forth at the original speed. Together we rocked and rocked and rocked. We rocked and rocked and rocked.

As we were rocking back and forth, I felt that we were one: united in pain, united in strength. I felt a sense of wholeness. I even felt some kind of holiness. I felt like Chico and I were pulsating with the entire universe. Was this what the whirling dervishes felt within the Muslim tradition? Was this what those "caught up in the spirit" felt within the Christian tradition? Was this what the Tai Chi masters felt within the Taoist tradition?

As crazy as I was, I experienced some healing that day. There was something Chico taught me that day. Did what he teach me have something to do with congruence, empathy, and unconditional positive regard? Something to do with being a wounded healer? Something about the spiritual model of care? Something about two becoming more than two?

When we become aware of our shared woundedness, our shared strengths, and the process of mutual healing, we can easily transition into empathy and unconditional positive regard. We can have respect for the feelings of others (have empathy) because we have respect for our own feelings; we can have unconditional positive regard for others because we have unconditional positive regard for ourselves. Empathy and unconditional positive regard can really become quite easy with the realization of our shared woundedness, our shared strengths, and the process of mutual healing.

As we nonjudgmentally welcome the various aspects of our own personalities, we prepare ourselves to nonjudgmentally welcome the various aspects of the personalities of others. In nonjudgmentally acknowledging and accepting my own shortcomings, I learn how to nonjudgmentally acknowledge and accept another's shortcomings. In nonjudgmentally acknowledging and accepting my own woundedness, I learn how to nonjudgmentally acknowledge and accept another's woundedness.

All of the above argument can be turned around also. When we are interested, attached, and concerned with others, we are, because of this truth of mutuality, interested, attached, and concerned with ourselves; in having compassion for others, we have compassion for ourselves. We are able to have a sense of healing when we can provide healing for others. This is what George Bach and Laura Torbet were saying when they said, "The Caring Paradox is that self-realization is only possible through caring for others. Caring for and about others is caring for ourselves. Caring for others accrues great benefits to us: it increases our self-esteem, attracts the care and concern of others, improves the environment, and enhances the quality of life. All caring is double-edged. We have impact on others by acknowledging their impact on us; we grow by supporting others' growth." [5]

One of the most difficult counseling cases I ever had happened in 1970. I was working out of a church in Washington D.C., a church that had a drug counseling service and a crisis hot line. I had just started a 2 a.m. shift on the telephones when a telephone call came in from a young woman named Suzi.

Suzi was seventeen years old. She had run away from her parents in Ohio eight months earlier. After living mostly in the streets and occasionally in a shared apartment with other "street people," she had gradually come to the resolve that she would return home to her parents. That resolve had been shattered when she discovered that she was pregnant; she felt her parents would certainly not welcome her if she returned home in that condition.

Suzi's pregnancy was the result of being raped. She had been raped several times during her life on the streets, rapes that she could not prevent or protest because she was a runaway without people or systems to be her advocates. Before calling the crisis hot line where I was working, she had attempted an abortion with pills and a coat hanger. She had apparently been bleeding terribly, and had now resolved to take her life. But before ending her life she wanted to express all the anger she felt; she wanted to tell the world how cruel it had been to her. That was the telephone call I received a little after I had started my shift at 2 a.m.; I was going to be the randomly chosen recipient of all of her anger.

Her hurt, her frustration, her sadness, her anger: it all spewed out over the telephone. She complained. She accused. She shouted. She cursed. She cried. She made me feel her hurt; I felt it. She made me feel her frustration; I felt it. She made me feel her sadness; I felt it. She made me feel her anger; I felt it.

After two and a half hours of Suzi expressing all of her emotions, the two of us entered a period of exhausted silence. She seemed very tired, very weak. She had said all she wanted to say and had not hung up; she was offering a space for some kind of response.

I asked for an update on her physical condition. She said she was no longer bleeding. She felt very weak and very tired. However, she wanted to talk some more.

We then spent the next two and a half hours sharing with one another. Although she kept repeating that she was utterly exhausted, she also repeatedly said that she wanted to continue talking. I too was utterly exhausted, but we talked and talked. We talked about everything: our likes and dislikes, our early childhoods, our parents, our favorite movies and favorite music. We even laughed a couple of times.

At a little after 7 a.m., Suzi said she needed to go to sleep. However, she promised me that she would first go to a hospital emergency room.

At the end of that evening I felt like I could also use some medical help. I was physically and emotionally spent. Yet, in the midst of that being spent, I was also somehow strangely energized, refreshed. I was reminded of when I was Suzi's age and had just finished a strenuous football game, taking that post-game shower, feeling all the aches and pain and exhaustion and yet also feeling relieved and revitalized.

Four weeks after that phone call, a young woman in a white dress walked into our counseling office and asked to see me. As soon as I heard her voice, I knew who she was. Suzi had come to say both "hello" and "goodbye:" she was going back to Ohio to see if her parents would take her back. We began talking again as if we had been the closest of friends for years. She told me that she was still very sad and very angry, but she was determined to not let either of those emotions get the better of her. She told me that she was no longer pregnant. We talked and talked.

As Suzi began to leave my office, she told me that she would never forget what she referred to as "our evening together." As she was leaving, she gave me a package. Inside the package was a small cross made out of nails and baling wire. I have used that cross many times as an object of meditation. It speaks of pain and it speaks of healing. It also speaks about mutuality, because whenever I meditate upon that cross, I remember a particular passage of Christian scripture: "I have been crucified with Christ; and it is no longer I who live, but Christ lives in me." [6] Shared wounds. Shared strengths. Shared healing.

The Buddhist Christine Longaker has said, "What makes us feel hopeless is not our difficult situation; it's being isolated in our suffering, fear or grief, and not being able to connect with others." [7] When we meet each other in relationships without dominance, without armor, in equal measures of humility and assertiveness, we connect with others and they connect with us. In that connection we experience congruence, empathy, and unconditional positive regard, sharing wounds, sharing strengths, sharing healing.

REFLECTION

Bring to mind what your motivations are for wanting to be someone's helper.

Write down (or verbally share) all the things you hope to give to those you are helping.

Write down (or verbally share) how the above list of things is similar to what you would like to receive as the result of being a helper.

REFLECTION

Write down (or verbally share) what you feel the dying most need.

Write down (or verbally share) what you feel the physically ill most need.

Write down (or verbally share) what you feel the emotionally ill most need.

Write down (or verbally share) what you feel the healthy most need.

Write down (or verbally share) what you feel you most need.

Write down (or verbally share) the similarities and differences found in your answers to the above questions.

Chapter Six
References

1. Deming, B. (1984). We Are All Part Of One Another. (J. Meyerding, Ed.). Gabriola Island, BC: New Society Publishers.

2. Cassidy, S. (1991). Sharing The Darkness. Maryknoll, NY: Orbis Books.

3. Wegela, K. K. (1996). How To Be A Help Instead Of A Nuisance. Boston: Shambhala.

4. Ram Dass & Gorman, P. (1985). How Can I Help?. New York: Alfred A. Knopf.

5. Bach, G. R., & Torbet, L. (1982). A Time For Caring. New York: Delacorte.

6. Galatians 2:20, New American Standard Bible.

7. Longaker, C. (1997). Facing Death And Finding Hope. New York: Doubleday.

Mutual Wounds

Those of us who work with the terminally ill have a continual awareness of that one particular wound that all of us most assuredly share: the wound of our common mortality. The fact that we all die is certainly a burden that has to be carried around with all of us, a wound that none of us can even hope to avoid. Although our mortality is certainly an inescapable wound, all around us we see various attempts at trying to escape it. We have trouble even mentioning the word "death" (e.g. she passed on, he kicked the bucket, she left us, he's gone over to the other side, she met her Maker, he's laid to rest, she's pushing up daisies, he bit the dust, she gave up the ghost, he was taken away, she's in the great beyond, he bought the farm, she's six feet under, he's a goner). In having all our euphemisms for death, we appear to have lost our awareness that it is a reality for all of us.

My work with the terminally ill has helped me to heighten my awareness of this important common wound. My work in hospice has also given me an even deeper awareness of woundedness in general, for the dying have all sorts of wounds. Sheila Cassidy acknowledged this deeper awareness when she said that "the hospice movement . . . affirms the value of the brain-damaged, the mutilated and the old to a world which values the clever, the physically beautiful and the athlete." [1] Hospice affirms the value of woundedness, the value of woundedness in general and the value of one particular universally shared wound, our inevitable death.

The modern loss of awareness of woundedness, especially our shared wound of death, is very different from the attitude present in our spiritual traditions. Many spiritual traditions have actually been founded upon, and centered around, the principle of facing the reality of death. It is the premise of these spiritual traditions that if we in fact face our woundedness (individual and mutual), especially facing death, we will end up leading a much fuller life than we normally do.

One present-day support for this premise that facing our wounds leads to a fuller life comes through all the recent studies of people who have had "near death experiences." Apparently, when people have somehow been revived after being on the brink of death, they have an almost universal response: they come out of that near death experience wanting to lead a more purposeful life. They come out of that experience with a renewed appreciation of life, an open and fearless relationship with death, and a commitment to finding more meaning in how they run their lives.

Our spiritual traditions make a similar claim: in no

longer fearing death, we have a renewed appreciation of life; life has an entirely different quality to it when we let go of our fears; there is purposefulness in life when we no longer fear death. Jesus probably had something of this in mind when he said that "unless a grain of wheat falls into the earth and dies, it remains by itself alone; but if it dies, it bears much fruit." [2] Bunan, the Buddhist teacher, probably had something of this in mind when he said, "While living be a dead man, be thoroughly dead — and behave as you like, and all's well." [3] This fuller life that comes through acknowledging our mortality is open to all of us because mortality is a wound that we all share; by acknowledging, experiencing, and working with our mortality (or any wound for that matter), we enter into the dimension of possible healing.

Rachel Naomi Remen has said that "at the heart of any real intimacy is a certain vulnerability. It is hard to trust someone with your vulnerability unless you can see in them a matching vulnerability and know that you will not be judged. In some basic way it is our imperfections and even our pain that draws others close to us." [4] In being effective helpers, our shared vulnerability and our shared woundedness must be present, internally acknowledged by ourselves and externally perceived by others.

Without our acknowledgment of mutual woundedness, our training, degrees, and experience will only help us to label and judge those placed in our care. However, that is not what people have come to us to receive. Those placed in our care, or those choosing to be in our care, do not want us to label and judge them; they want us to accept them for who they are and to provide them with healing. Their assurance that we will not label and judge them can only come from the fact that our woundedness is mutual, internally acknowledged by ourselves and externally perceived by them. In perceiving this position of mutuality, those that come into our care can be assured that we will not label and judge them, because in labeling and judging them, we will be labeling and judging ourselves. Through a recognition of mutual woundedness, we can provide an atomosphere of non-judging and non-labeling, a safe haven, a sanctuary for healing.

This recognition of mutual woundedness has to be accompanied by the additional recognition that each of us experiences that common woundedness in a unique way and we need to accept and respect each other's unique way of experiencing that woundedness. Because I have lost a child to death does not mean that I can completely understand other people's suffering due to the loss of a child: I must accept and respect each person's unique form of that suffering. Because I have had mental illness does not mean that I can completely understand other people's suffering from mental illness: I must accept and respect each person's unique form of that suffering. Because I have had a divorce does not mean that I can completely understand other people's suffering from divorce: I must accept and respect each person's unique form of that suffering. This acceptance and respect for someone else's unique form of woundedness is a necessary part of our empathy and unconditional positive regard. Without that full acceptance and respect, there is only sympathy, not empathy.

Helen Perlman has voiced a concern regarding people who have sympathy but no empathy. She has said, "There is probably no more annoying or even threatening person than one who *understands* too quickly and too deeply, before you have had a chance to get the words out of your mouth, who reassures too swiftly because of his sometimes erroneous assumption that you and he are on the same wavelength. Such a person may often make a quite different interpretation of what you said from what you meant. Such a person may be quite sympathetic, bent on making you feel better fast. But he is not empathic." [5] This is one of the reasons why I mentioned earlier that empathy keeps us from rushing in with quick and easy answers to people's problems. For us to be empathic and have unconditional positive regard, we need to have a quiet, receptive respect, a reverence, for someone's unique form of our mutual woundedness.

With this quiet, receptive respect, we present a safe haven, a sanctuary, a place where people can openly share their wounds. When people experience our quiet, receptive respect, they know we have empathy and unconditional positive regard; they know we are healers.

My dad helped me understand this concept of establishing a safe haven, a sanctuary. In our relationship, we eventually got to the point where we could discuss our mutual woundedness and have respect for each other's specifically unique forms of that woundedness. However, the beginning of our relationship could hardly be described as a safe haven or sanctuary; the beginning of our relationship could only be described as a relationship of dominance.

When I was young, I perceived my dad through a very limited perspective. Much of the relationship centered around my fear of him; his presence always seemed quite threatening. As I was growing up, he was always considerably larger than I, even when I was in high school and college. As I was growing up, I never saw him cry, never heard him express words of love, never saw him hug or kiss my mom, never saw or heard him communicate anything that might give anyone the impression that he was not completely self-sufficient, not in need of anyone or anything.

Throughout our early relationship, I usually just kept a safe distance from him. We might occasionally talk to one another, but we would never approach topics that could involve any emotional depth. We might occasionally do things together, but nothing that would not fit within my dad's tightly defined image, not much beyond watching a football game, playing pool on our pool table, or working on the lawn.

As a consequence of this upbringing, I was never aware of any woundedness that my dad might have; I did not see him as having any vulnerability; I did not imagine that he had any shortcomings or weaknesses. As a result of my dad's attitude, I never wanted to confess my own woundedness, my own vulnerability, my own shortcomings and weaknesses; my dad's wearing of armor before me elicited my own wearing of armor before him.

The above described relationship between my dad and I was without interruption until I was well into my twenties. The relationship began to change the day that my daughter Kristin died (her story is told later in this book). On that day I had called my parents from the hospital informing them of her death, saying that I was driving over to see them. When I pulled into the driveway of their house, I saw my dad walking out the front door. He walked up to me as I was getting out of the car, came face-to-face with me, and stood in front of me long enough for me to see tears welling up in his eyes: he did not want me to see him cry, but he wanted me to know he was going to cry. He then turned around and marched back into the house, slamming the door as he entered. When I was inside the house, I could hear him sobbing behind his bedroom door. That day I realized that my dad knew woundedness; that day our relationship made some considerable progress towards becoming a relationship without dominance, a relationship where there might be hope for eliminating much of the armor that existed between us.

The relationship took another giant step forward on the day of my brother Dean's funeral. My other brothers and I were gathered inside my parents' house. My dad came up to me and asked me to follow him into the back yard. As I was following him into the back yard, he was showing me many things that he had planted (all of which I had seen on previous visits). He kept walking further and further into the yard, finally stopping at the furthest corner of the yard, a corner that was not visible from inside the house. When we arrived at that corner of the yard, he took ahold of my shoulders, looked me in the eyes, and said, "Doug, I loved your brother and I love you." He then wrapped his arms around me and started crying, his belly and great bulk shaking convulsively as he cried. In showing me that vulnerability, he made me feel very close to him, very close; at that moment, I sensed some deep healing occurring for him, for me, and for us.

Our developing relationship of closeness grew some more after I was released from the mental hospital. At the same time, my dad realized that he was close to death, having a combination of a damaged heart, emphysema, cancer, and an addiction to steroids. During his final days, we lived in the same town, many of those days living together in the same house. We shared much during that time, much about our shared humanness, our disappointments, our common longings, and our mutual wounds. It was during this time that we developed a great deal of respect for one another, a respect that grew naturally out of our shared humanness, our shared disappointments, our shared common longings, and our mutual wounds. My seeing of my dad in all of his vulnerability caused me to respect him as I had never before respected him. He must have been having similar feelings for me as he witnessed my vulnerability.

Once respect for our unique forms of woundedness entered into our relationship, empathy and unconditional positive regard were right there as well. With empathy and unconditional positive regard, healing took place. Yes, my dad died (nothing could have stopped that), but I really believe he experienced some healing in those final months. Although he was certainly frustrated and angry about all the problems and losses he was having because of his various maladies, he also was experiencing some real healing: he discovered his family's love for him (rather than our fear); he discovered some new things about our father-son relationship (and his other father-son relationships); he had a type of psycho-spiritual transformation that took the form of an appreciation of classical music (especially Respighi's "Fountains of Rome"); he let go of many of his fears, especially his fear of being emotionally honest. He learned much about the true values of life: sharing, caring, loving, mutual wounds, mutual strengths, mutual healing.

As I have said both implicitly and explicitly, many people in this world are investing a lot of energy in unrealistic hopes, hoping that some man or woman, guru or messiah, event or encounter, will magically eliminate all their wounds. These are unrealistic hopes.

As helpers, we cannot offer people a cure for all woundedness; woundedness will always be with us. However, we can offer healing in the midst of that woundedness, offering congruence, empathy, and unconditional positive regard. We can offer the message that people need not run away from their wounds, they need not hide from their wounds, they need not pretend that their wounds do not exist.

We must not be in the business of offering a problem-free life: there can be no such thing. We must all appreciate the mystery and usefulness of suffering. We must respect our woundedness, our mutual woundedness. As Henri Nouwen has said, "Shared pain is no longer paralysing. . . . When we become aware that we do not have to escape our pains, but that we can mobilize them into a common search for life, those very pains are transformed from expressions of despair into signs of hope." [7]

In some of the oldest spiritual traditions, the existence of shamans witnessed to the importance of shared wounds. The shamans were the true experts in healing: they were a combination doctor and spiritual advisor. They were experts in healing because they were experts in knowing their own woundedness and in sharing in the woundedness of others. Shamans, in their typical practice, completely entered into the world of the person in need of healing, entering into the very midst of the sickness to lead the person on a mutual journey back to health. The shaman was someone with direct experience of woundedness, someone who had previously traveled the road from sickness to health. This familiarity with woundedness was the shaman's most important qualification and credential.

The modern medical doctor's qualifications and credentials are very different from the shaman's. The modern doctor does not even have to have any personal experience with woundedness; a doctor can claim to be an expert in healing without ever having to acknowledge sickness in his or her own life, without ever even acknowledging that he or she shares in the woundedness of all of humanity. Such a doctor could perhaps produce some "cures" through book knowledge. However, such a doctor would have a very difficult time in showing congruence and empathy, thus having a very difficult time in providing people with "healing."

Many modern psychotherapists also have very different qualifications and credentials from the shaman's, much different styles of practicing as well. The modern emphasis on "clinical distance" is not like the style of the shaman, hardly the practice of someone with congruence, empathy, and unconditional positive regard.

Many modern clergy follow the same route as many modern medical doctors and many modern psychotherapists, claiming to be "called apart" for the ministry, situating themselves (as I situated myself) in some lonely mid-zone between the people and who the people worship. Whereas the medical doctor practices separation through book knowledge, drugs, diagnostic tests, and elaborate machines, the minister practices separation through piety, vestments, pulpits, and altar rails. Once again: an avoidance of mutuality, and thus an avoidance of congruence, empathy, and unconditional positive regard.

We, as people wanting to be genuine helpers, must reverse this modern trend and get back to the healing messages incorporated in our spiritual traditions, giving at least equal credence to the spiritual model as to the medical model. We have to realize, as Kat Duff realized, that "in our attempt to banish illnesses from the world, we banish the knowledge that can save us. . . . [We] have to learn . . . from our illnesses and the sacred spaces we inhabit in pain." [8] We need to learn how to acknowledge, approach, and use our mutual woundedness.

In finding the place of our shared woundedness, and in respecting that place, respecting everyone's unique form of that mutual woundedness, we will open ourselves up to share in our mutual strengths and mutual healing. As Albert Kreinheder has said, "The greatest treasure comes out of the most despised and secret places. . . . This place of greatest vulnerability is also a holy place, a place of healing." [9]

REFLECTION

Write down (or verbally share) what you feel was meant by Henri Nouwen when he said, "Shared pain is no longer paralyzing."

REFLECTION

Write down (or verbally share) a description of a person who is in your life (or has been in your life) who has provided you with a "safe haven," a place where you can be your true self with all your shortcomings, pain, and woundedness.

What qualities do (did) you most appreciate in this person?

How is (was) this person's congruency, authenticity, shown to you?

How does (did) this person show empathy towards you?

How does (did) this person show unconditional positive regard for you?

REFLECTION

Read, read again, and meditate upon the following:

"Reclaiming ourselves usually means coming to recognize and accept that we have in us both sides of everything. We are capable of fear and courage, generosity and selfishness, vulnerability and strength. These things do not cancel each other out but offer us a full range of power and response to life. Life is as complex as we are. Sometimes our vulnerability is our strength, our fear develops our courage, and our woundedness is the road to our integrity. It is not an either/or world." [10]

REFLECTION

Read, read again, and meditate upon the following:

"We are all frail people, vulnerable and wounded; it is just that some of us are more clever at concealing it than others!" [11]

REFLECTION

Read, read again, and meditate upon the following:

"Suffering shapes the life force, sometimes into anger, sometimes into blame and self-pity. Eventually it may show us the freedom of loving and serving life." [12]

REFLECTION

Read, read again, and meditate upon the following:

"Every time I am forced by circumstances or my own stupidity to enter into darkness and suffering I emerge battered, but richer." [13]

Chapter Seven
References

1. Cassidy, S. (1991). Sharing The Darkness. Maryknoll, NY: Orbis Books.

2. John 12:24, New American Standard Bible.

3. quoted in Philip Kapleau's The Wheel Of Life And Death. (1989). New York: Doubleday.

4. Remen, R. N. (1994). Kitchen Table Wisdom. New York: Riverhead Books.

5. Perlman, H. H. (1979). Relationship: The Heart Of Helping People. Chicago: University of Chicago Press.

6. John 19:6, King James Bible.

7. Nouwen, H. J. M. (1972). The Wounded Healer. New York: Doubleday.

8. Duff, K. (1993). The Alchemy Of Illness. New York: Pantheon Books.

9. Kreinheder, A. (1991). Body And Soul: The Other Side Of Illness. Toronto: Inner City Books.

10. Remen, R. N. (1996). Kitchen Table Wisdom. New York: Riverhead Books.

11. Cassidy, S. (1991). Sharing The Darkness. Maryknoll, NY: Orbis Books.

12. Remen, R. N. (1996). Kitchen Table Wisdom. New York: Riverhead Books.

13. Cassidy, S. (1991). Sharing The Darkness. Maryknoll, NY: Orbis Books.

Mutual Strengths

We have all heard the maxim that "two heads are better than one." Are not two sets of hands better than one also? Are not two hearts better than one? What about two spirits?

The transformation from woundedness to healing has to usually get beyond our mere acknowledgment of our own suffering and the suffering of others. Sharing our common suffering and respecting each other's unique form of that suffering certainly can provide some people with comfort and provide them with a safe haven whereby they can start to grow beyond their suffering: for some people that is really all they want and need. However, for many people, there is the additional need to pool our strengths after the safe haven has been established. For many people, there needs to be a realization of "mutual strength," the realization that we are all valuable and our values commingle: we can grow through the pooling of our strengths.

There is power in sharing strengths. What we might fear to do on our own, we can often do with little fear if there is someone with us. What we feel we cannot bear on our own, we can often bear with the help of others. What we feel we cannot accomplish on our own, we can often accomplish if someone is just beside us. Our wounds can experience healing through the strengths we receive from others and with others.

The birth and death of my first child, Kristin, taught me much about the value of mutual strengths. Recovering from the death of a child often takes more strength than can be had by a single individual. For me, to begin the healing process in the midst of that death, I needed to rely on the strengths of others, several others.

Kristin was a premature child, being born about seven weeks premature. She came into this world with several internal malformations: four kidneys rather than two, a defective heart, probable brain damage, and several other problems. She also had some very unusual external traits: extremely pale skin, very long black hair, and eyes that were almost black in color, eyes that often rolled up into her head, leaving only the whites behind. Her cry was unusual as well, very high-pitched and eerie sounding, sometimes sounding as if it was not coming from her, but from some distant place behind her or above her.

Immediately after being delivered, Kristin was flown from the hospital of her birth to another hospital fifty miles away, a hospital with an intensive care unit for newborns. Before Kristin was taken from my wife and I, we baptized her with our own tears. More tears came as we left the hospital, my wife being taken out of the hospital in a wheelchair, carrying flowers instead of a child.

What followed was a very grueling seven weeks of one hope being dashed after another: excitement every time that Kristin gained an ounce, despair when that one ounce gain was followed by a two ounce loss. During those seven weeks, our suffering was shared by many people: other parents of newborns at that same hospital, our own parents, friends, co-workers, ministers, even strangers who somehow heard of our plight. As we waited, we received cards, telephone calls, visits: people not knowing exactly what to say, but all offering their support in whatever way they could.

One person who was especially supportive was a Dr. Albers, a cardiologist. He talked with us, occasionally held our hands, occasionally gave us hugs. He was also the person to inform us that Kristin needed heart surgery; he told us that he was going to have to operate on Kristin, telling us that the operation would have only a five percent chance of success, but without the operation Kristin would soon die. After the operation, when Kristin did die, Dr. Albers was also the person who came to us and said, "We have lost *our* daughter." Then he cried with us.

Very few people can bear the burden of losing a child all alone; it is often just too much to bear for only one person (or even a couple). But my wife and I were not alone, not alone at all. We were allowed to share in the strengths of others. The other parents there, who were sharing in our suffering, gave us strength that could only come from people who were traveling a very similar journey. Our own parents, who were also sharing in our suffering, gave us strength that could have only come from someone who knew all of our emotional history. Our friends, who were also sharing in our suffering, gave us some additional strength, strength that was very different from the strengths we received from those other parents of ailing newborns and our own parents. Co-workers, ministers, and strangers, who were also sharing in our suffering, gave us strength just by trying extra hard to say and do the right thing, and Dr. Albers, who also shared in our suffering, gave us a very special strength.

Alone, we would have had a very difficult time surviving emotionally. However, we were not alone. We participated in some mutual strengths, mutual strengths that allowed us to not just survive but also experience some very real healing.

I have found that when people look back upon their past experiences of being in helping relationships, no matter what side of the helping relationship they might have been on, they can easily see how strengths were shared back and forth. Ministers can make lay people feel strong; lay people can make ministers feel strong. Doctors can make patients feel strong; patients can make doctors feel strong. Psychotherapists can make clients feel strong; clients can make psychotherapists feel strong. This was perceived by Ram Dass and Paul Gorman when they said, "We work on ourselves . . . in order to help others. And we help others as a vehicle for working on ourselves." [1]

All of the teachers, supervisors, and counselors who inspired us to grow personally and professionally were probably themselves growing people, people who were accustomed to healing their own woundedness. Their personal growth was contagious: all personal growth is contagious.

When we do any kind of counseling, we realize over and over that helping others to grow contributes to our own continuing growth. Helping others to feel strong, makes us feel strong; we have a combined strength established through the sharing of our individual strengths; we have a mutual strength, a strength coming through our mutuality.

I remember Michael. He was born in the same month and year that I was born. I had always had difficulty in working with the dying when they were close to my age: I would then, more than at other times, be aware of the truth that our roles could easily be reversed. This feeling was very much present when I was working with Michael.

Michael was in dire straits. He had lung cancer. He weighed a little less than one hundred and twenty pounds. He had been homeless for the last ten years, losing his last job because of an alcohol problem. After being diagnosed with the lung cancer, his ex-wife felt sorry for him and invited him to move in with her, her current husband, and a son born to her and Michael.

I remember the day that I was assessing Michael, especially the moment when I asked him his age. Before asking him his age, I was under the impression that he was at least fifteen or twenty years older than I. However, when I heard his birth date, my heart literally "went out to him:" that could be me in that bed. I could have been Michael, in that place, with that disease, with that history, facing that death.

Because of my emotional attachment to Michael, I wanted to visit him daily rather than just my usual twice-a-week visits. I did manage to visit him with such frequency that there was never more than a day between my visits, even though that often meant visiting him in the evening and on weekends. Throughout the beginning of our relationship, I would feel poorly when Michael was feeling poorly, feeling my health being affected by his health. And although I was working for hospice, I wanted to step out of that hospice role with Michael; I did not want to help facilitate Michael's death; I wanted to postpone Michael's death.

Michael had to be the one to remind me of my job; he had to remind me that he was in fact dying. As he was reminding me of that, he was giving me strength, the strength I needed to come to terms with my own death, the strength that I was supposed to be giving him. At first, the strength that was shared between us was coming mostly from him to me, then gradually it changed so that it was mostly coming from me to him. Sometimes it was both of us giving strength to each other simultaneously. We were a partnership, functioning together, feeding on each other's strengths, having a common strength, a mutual strength.

I remember my last day with Michael, the day before he died; he died on one of the days between my visits. As I was ending the last visit I had with him, he said something I will always remember. We had only known each other for nine weeks. However, as I was leaving, that day before he died, he smiled as he said, “Doug, it’s been a long, long road we’ve been traveling, hasn’t it?”

Michael reinforced a message I need to hear over and over again: we are complex people, very complex, but never self-sufficient; we need others. We need them when we are suffering; we need them when we are not suffering. We need them in the beginning of life, in the middle, and especially in the end.

As people wanting to help others, we have probably all had experiences where we have gained courage to face our own problems from the courage we have seen in the people we have been trying to help. We have also probably gained a peace of mind in the midst of turmoil because of the peace of mind we have seen in those same people.

I remember Wilma. She had a cancer that had eaten away at her face. The only part of her face that looked "normal" was half of her forehead, the rest of her face was severely stripped of skin, exposing what was below the skin with all the ravaging that the cancer was dealing out. The physical and psychological pain of such a condition was obviously devastating. However, Wilma found joy in life. She greeted me everyday with some uplifting comment. She offered emotional support for her husband as he took on the many duties of being her caregiver. She expressed heartfelt thanksgiving for the smallest of favors that anyone offered her.

Wilma was manifesting a strength that she gave to others. Wilma was manifesting unconditional positive regard for her caregivers and was helping us have unconditional positive regard for her. Wilma's strength became a mutual strength. Her strength fed our strength, and then our strength built to feed her strength: the strength grew in the sharing.

With this topic of mutual strength, we see a repeat of a previous observance: modern psychotherapy (using the medical model) falls short in emphasizing this phenomenon whereas the emphasis in the spiritual traditions (the spiritual model) is quite evident. Much of modern psychotherapy is very individualistic, promoting individual assertiveness, looking out for "number one" (the number one being the individual's own self). On the other hand, the spiritual traditions emphasize the power of fellowship, the power of mutual strength: the two or three gathered in Christianity, the Sangha in Buddhism, and the combining of seeming opposites in Taoism.

There is power in togetherness; there is power in community. There is strength in fellowship, whether that fellowship involve the whole world, a nation, or simply three people, or even two. When we have empathy and unconditional positive regard for one another, we experience that strength, our mutual strength. As Ram Dass and Paul Gorman have reminded us: "How much we can get back in giving! How much we can offer in the way we receive? . . . Where does one begin, the other end? They seem to be happening simultaneously." [2]

REFLECTION

Bring to mind a death (or other loss experience: job loss, divorce, serious illness) that has occurred in your family.

Write down (or verbally share) the strengths that others provided to you during that time, strengths that you felt were lacking in yourself.

REFLECTION

Bring to mind some people to whom you have shown unconditional positive regard.

Write down (or verbally share) what they have gained from you.

Write down (or verbally share) what you have gained from them.

Bring to mind some people who have shown unconditional positive regard towards you.

Write down (or verbally share) what you have gained from them.

Write down (or verbally share) what they have gained from you.

REFLECTION

Read, read again, and meditate upon the following:

"When experiencing difficulty in discerning your own needs, it may be helpful to begin by observing what you provide for others. Often we give to other people what we unconsciously know that we need ourselves." [3]

REFLECTION

Read, read again, and meditate upon the following:

"The world is not divided into the sick and those who care for them, but that we are all wounded and that we all contain within our hearts that love which is for the healing of the nations. What we lack is the courage to start giving it away." [4]

Chapter Eight
References

1. Ram Dass & Gorman, P. (1985). How Can I Help?. New York: Alfred A. Knopf.

2. Ram Dass & Gorman, P. (1985). How Can I Help?. New York: Alfred A. Knopf.

3. Berry, C. R. (1988). When Helping You Is Hurting Me. New York: Harper & Row.

4. Cassidy, S. (1991). Sharing The Darkness. Maryknoll, NY: Orbis Books.

Mutual Healing And The Wounded Healer

Kahlil Gibran offered the following parable portraying the wounded healer motif:

"Said one oyster to a neighboring oyster, 'I have a very great pain within me. It is heavy and round and I am in distress.'

"And the other oyster replied with haughty complacence, 'Praise be to the heavens and to the sea, I have no pain within me. I am well and whole both within and without.'

"At that moment a crab was passing by and heard the two oysters, and he said to the one who was well and whole both within and without, 'Yes, you are well and whole; but the pain that your neighbor bears is a pearl of exceeding beauty.'" [1]

The imagery of how a pearl is formed was often used in the psycho-spiritual writings of the alchemists. The alchemists used this image as a way of describing the transformation of a psycho-physical hardship into a psycho-spiritual treasure. The goal of the alchemical/psycho-spiritual process was to produce the "priceless" pearl of transformation, spiritual transformation. For the alchemist, we merely need to start with a troublesome irritant, a physical malady or a psychological disturbance, and daily work on that malady/disturbance. Through daily work with that troublesome irritant, we gradually "polish" the malady or disturbance, gradually changing it so that one day it becomes a pearl. Yet, its true value does not become evident until it is somehow literally "fished up" from the very depths of our being and literally "pried loose" from us. After the irritant-now-become-a-pearl is brought into the "light," it is then "worn" on the warm skin which allows it to keep its "luster." What was once hidden and despised is now publically shown and valued; what was once an individual's wound is now for the healing of many.

An important thing to remember in this process is the value of the irritant. Without the irritant, there could be no pearl. Attempting to rid ourselves of all of our irritants creates the possibility of ridding ourselves of "priceless" psycho-spiritual treasures. As Kat Duff has said, "When problems are quickly solved and we return to our old selves, the questions illnesses inevitably raise — and the insights and opportunities they offer — are erased and nullified. We have developed so many tools, from visualizations to painkillers, for suppressing symptoms and their accompanying question marks that we have lost the ability to come to terms with pain and suffering, to be changed, informed, and even illuminated by their presence in our lives." [2]

In doing seminars on the topic of being a wounded healer, I try to share my woundedness in such a way that I can help others in their healing process. When I make that my primary goal I find that such sharing helps me in my healing process as well.

When I, in aiming to help others heal, share my experiences around the death of my daughter, I find myself also receiving some healing. Almost always after sharing my story, I will have a couple people come up to me, thank me for my story, and then proceed to tell me their stories of losing a child or a grandchild. And, in hearing their stories, I am helped along in my healing process.

Whenever I, in aiming to help others heal, share my experiences about my being institutionalized in the mental hospital, I find myself also receiving some healing. Almost always after sharing my story, I will have a couple people come up to me, thank me for my story, and then proceed to tell me about their own process of healing: a healing from some other struggle with organized religion, a healing from some psychological problem, or a healing from some other experience of being institutionalized. And, when they share with me about their own healing, that, in turn, further helps me in my healing.

This is mutual healing. In helping to heal others, I am given some healing.

When we are wounded, the wound in us evokes the

healer in those who care for us. When we evoke the healer in someone, we provide them with a boost in their self-esteem (some healing for them). When we are trying to be healers, the wounds in those we care for evoke our own healing qualities, providing us with a boost in our self-esteem (some healing for us). In respectfully giving, we receive; in respectfully receiving, we give.

There is a great amount of pleasure received in giving someone useful knowledge, a pleasure equal to receiving useful knowledge. There is a great amount of pleasure received in giving someone words that comfort, a pleasure equal to receiving comfortable words. There is a great amount of pleasure received in giving someone some welcomed physical assistance, a pleasure equal to receiving that welcomed assistance. In respectfully giving, we receive. The best of healing involves a "mutual" healing.

What we learn from people who have lost their jobs is to truly cherish our own. What we learn from people who have lost their sight is to truly cherish our own. What we learn from people who have lost a child is to truly cherish our own. What we learn from people who have lost their lives is to truly cherish our own.

In my work with the dying, I have listened to many people as they have come to the end of life's journey. As I mentioned in the beginning of this book, I have learned much from them, knowledge I could not get any place else. From them I have learned much about how precious each breath can be, how wonderful it is to have people that love you, how delicious a cup of coffee can be, how fortunate it is to be without pain. I, through the dying, have learned much about the details of life, looking and really seeing, listening and really hearing, touching and really feeling. I, through the dying, have learned much about not wasting the precious gift of time. I, through the dying, have learned much about lessening the amount of "musts" and "shoulds" and focusing more on real "needs," my own real needs and the real needs of others. I, through the dying, have learned much about building courage, realizing that what I used to think of as challenging and/or frightening is really not that challenging or frightening. I, through the dying, have learned much about seeking "meaning" and "purpose" in my life, wanting to leave this world a little better than I found it. I, through the dying, have learned much about acknowledging that my own life will come to an end and how important it is for me to acknowledge that and fully live whatever life I have left. I, through the dying, have learned much about a deeper spiritual consciousness, realizing that our world is so much more than what we can touch, see, and measure. All of those lessons that come from the dying are healing messages, healing received from the wounded, healing that comes from wounded healers.

Remember Bob Blanchard, the man who provided healing for some students who felt mentally inadequate. He congruently lived and breathed physical and mental achievement. He empathically related to the shortcomings of others. He showed unconditional positive regard for a motley crew of young men, young men who had yet to realize their potential, young men who discovered their potential through Bob's congruence, empathy, and unconditional positive regard.

Remember how one Episcopal priest named Doug lost everything he had by perpetuating a relationship of dominance. He failed to value congruence, empathy, and unconditional positive regard. He took power, abused that power, and brought down himself and many others in the process. Yet, he eventually found some healing through the accepting and acknowledging of his own vulnerability, his own woundedness.

Remember a man named Tom, who, although dying, experienced some healing by letting go of some armor. He grew from exposing his vulnerability.

Remember Frank and Mildred holding hands, knowing how we truly share in one another's lives.

Remember Chico rocking back and forth in a mental hospital. Although he had been labeled "mentally ill," he knew much about the spiritual model of care and how we heal in the midst of our woundedness, healing in our togetherness.

Remember seventeen year old Suzi living on the

streets of Washington D.C.. She was terribly wounded, yet she was a wonderful healer.

Remember how we are all members of the same family, all in this world together, all wounded, all capable of receiving and giving healing. Remember how we all share in one another's woundedness and in one another's healing. Remember how we can all be wounded healers.

Buddhism teaches that I, just as I am, am the Buddha, and that everyone I meet, just as they are, are also the Buddha; that is enlightenment. I, in all my woundedness, am the Buddha. Others, in all their woundedness, are the Buddha. I, just as I am, have the power to heal and the power to experience healing. Others, just as they are, have the power to heal and the power to experience healing.

Within the Judeo-Christian tradition there is the belief that I, just as I am, am made in the image of God: I am a "temple" in which God dwells. Also, others, just as they are, are made in the image of God: they too are "temples" in which God dwells. We, in all our woundedness have within us the very being of God; we have within us the power to heal and the power to experience healing.

Rachel Naomi Remen has said, "It's our woundedness that allows us to trust each other. I can trust another person only if I can sense that they, too, have woundedness, have pain, have fear. Out of that trust we can begin to pay attention to our own wounds and to each other's wounds - and to heal and be healed." [3]

Chapter Nine
References

1.. Gibran, K. (1932). The Wanderer. New York: Alfred A. Knopf.

2. Duff, K. (1993). The Alchemy Of Illness. New York: Pantheon Books.

3. Remen, R.N. (1993). "Wholeness" in Bill Moyers, Healing And The Mind. New York: Doubleday.

The Author

Douglas C. Smith, MA, MS, MDiv, has masters degrees in three different disciplines – believing strongly in a holistic perspective. However, he feels that his most important education has come outside of the classroom: the death of his daughter, his stay as a patient in a mental hospital, his being deposed as a priest, and his ten years experience in working with the dying. Doug brings both this academic background and this experiential knowledge to his current work as an author, seminar leader, and health care consultant.

Doug's Seminars

Doug does several seminars for health care employees and the general public. Among those seminars are the following:

"Final Rights: Caring for People in the Final Phases of Life"

"Exploring and Enhancing Spirituality: How to Care for the Spiritual Needs of the Sick, Dying, and Bereaved"

"Putting the Care Back into Health Care"

"Being a Wounded Healer: How to be a Caring and Effective Helper."

For more information on Doug's seminars, you can contact him by phone at (608) 231-1541 or by e-mail at dougcsmith@juno.com. Or you can learn more about his seminars, including ones that might be already scheduled in your area, by calling Carondelet Management and the American Academy of Bereavement at (800) 726-3888.